Terrors of Childhood in Grimms' Fairy Tales

BERKELEY INSIGHTS IN LINGUISTICS AND SEMIOTICS

Irmengard Rauch
General Editor

Vol. 53

PETER LANG
New York • Washington, D.C./Baltimore • Bern
Frankfurt am Main • Berlin • Brussels • Vienna • Oxford

W. G. Kudszus

Terrors of Childhood
in Grimms' Fairy Tales

PETER LANG
New York • Washington, D.C./Baltimore • Bern
Frankfurt am Main • Berlin • Brussels • Vienna • Oxford

Library of Congress Cataloging-in-Publication Data

Kudszus, Winfried.
Terrors of childhood in Grimms' fairy tales / W. G. Kudszus.
p. cm. — (Berkeley insights in linguistics and semiotics; v. 53)
Includes bibliographical references and index.
1. Grimm, Jacob, 1785–1863—Criticism and interpretation.
2. Grimm, Wilhelm, 1786–1859—Criticism and interpretation.
3. Kinder- und Hausmärchen. 4. Fairy tales—Germany—History and criticism.
5. Childhood in literature. I. Title. II. Series.
PT921.K84   398.2'092'243—dc21   2002022499
ISBN 0−8204−5055−1
ISSN 0893−6935

Bibliographic information published by **Die Deutsche Bibliothek**.
Die Deutsche Bibliothek lists this publication in the "Deutsche
Nationalbibliografie"; detailed bibliographic data is available
on the Internet at http://dnb.ddb.de/.

The paper in this book meets the guidelines for permanence and durability
of the Committee on Production Guidelines for Book Longevity
of the Council of Library Resources.

© 2005 Peter Lang Publishing, Inc., New York
275 Seventh Avenue, 28th Floor, New York, NY 10001
www.peterlangusa.com

All rights reserved.
Reprint or reproduction, even partially, in all forms such as microfilm,
xerography, microfiche, microcard, and offset strictly prohibited.

Printed in Germany

For Olivia, Julian, Anya, and Nina

At this moment, an odd event took place in the young man's brain: the stones spoke to him, not out of his memory of having seen them so often; but in an undefinable manner, they seemed to be charged for him with an obscure message, translatable as either *yes* or *no*.

—JULIEN GREEN
Si j'étais vous…

Contents

Acknowledgments	xi
1 In the Beginning	1
2 *Brüder Grimm:* Der König vom goldenen Berg	4
The King of the Golden Mountain	5
3 A Yearning at the Heart of Terror: Language and Psyche in "The King of the Golden Mountain"	15
4 *Brüder Grimm:* Der gläserne Sarg	32
The Glass Coffin	33
5 Skins of a Tale: "The Glass Coffin"	45
6 Between Dream and Wakefulness: The Female Protagonist in "The Glass Coffin"	61
7 *Brüder Grimm:* Der treue Johannes	72
Faithful Johannes	73
8 The Idiom of Passion: "Faithful Johannes"	87
9 *Brüder Grimm:* Von dem Machandelboom	100
The Juniper Tree	101
10 Eating and Giving Birth: "The Juniper Tree"	117
11 Ending	131
Notes	135
References	139
Index	143

Acknowledgments

While the Grimm tales have been with me longer than I am able to remember, the beginnings of this particular study date from an enchanted stay in Catalonia—Girona—with Francine and our son, Julian, who just then began to speak. I thank him for his words, emerging as they did from the several tongues that surrounded us, and for treating me to sounds with fresh, often mysterious significations. I thank Francine for her encouragement to pursue the questions before you, for her literary evocations, and for simply—inexplicably—being there.

Casey Butterfield gave my text a poet's reading and an exquisitely detailed response. Mary Cudahy's kindred perceptions offered intellectually and experientially illuminating contexts for my thoughts on early childhood. Irmgart Noack elucidated intricately regional Pomeranian and Hamburgian idioms for the translation of "The Juniper Tree." The Semiotic Circle of California continues to provide my explorations with a uniquely resonant forum: there and elsewhere Irmengard Rauch's semiotic sophistication beyond compare, and Alain Cohen's breathtaking semio-psychoanalytic acumen have energized my efforts. I am grateful as well to the students of my Berkeley fairy tale seminars who involved their hearts and minds in our proceedings. I wish to thank Lihua Zhang for her most knowledgeable support in computer matters, and Maria Amoroso at Lang New York for her dedicated and efficient production work. Symposia in Palermo, Vienna, Perpignan, Barcelona, and Cologne allowed me to present my considerations before committing them to print.

Before and beyond words, my children, Olivia, Julian, Anya, and Nina, have inspired and informed the spirit of these pages.

1
In the Beginning

> My frozen words
> have thawed
> flow through alien lands...
>
> ROSE AUSLÄNDER
> *Dem Meer zu*

The boundary at which we begin to speak constitutes a momentous beginning from which we go on, with unprecedented vigor, to transform relatively fluid experiences into units with particular names and faces. But in a crucial sense there is no such beginning; only in retrospect—along developmental, ideological, and analytically explorative lines—can we speak of a boundary that was reached and crossed at the time. If we forgo the perspectives and the linear narratives that place the past into an interpretive relationship with the present or future, a dramatically changed and charged story emerges. Certainly this story can, and often begs, to be linked to subsequent events; for the time being, however, it calls for recognition on its own grounds.[1]

The idiom of a time that was experienced in its immediacy, in its freedom and playfulness, inspires and haunts the tales in the study before you. How might this language of times past become audible, buried as it is under the ruling words and plots?[2] Language in the beginning: with each new word—we imagine—there is a certain loss of the richly evocative life that preceded it.[3] Something is now more clearly delineated than it was before. Barely learned, but available for usage from now on, that something leaves one's mouth, making sounds that refer to particular people and objects. Others manufacture these things called words as well. Defined linguistic communication has begun.

For a while such words are much like playthings. They can be tossed back and forth, and they can be felt and tasted, when you speak them while eating, or mix them with a bit of saliva as they roll off your lips.[4] As time passes, however, words become more focused business. Cleanly formed, correctly pronounced, and dryly released, they are the privileged coinage of human communication and individual progress. Having been assigned their correct spots in the larger context of the sentence, they gradually—and necessarily, it seems—enter into vast networks of signification.

While a sense of play and nascency may survive in the course of such a development, individual origins of language elude conscious recall. At the same time, we may feel a lack of depth and of a sense of authenticity when using language in its given manifestations. Indeed, the very words available to us on the theme of our linguistic origins block a more engaged approach; are we not employing decidedly adult terms in pursuit of childhood beginnings?[5] References to a lack of depth, for example, can be expected to lose their usefulness on the way back to those origins. A broader phenomenon appears in the realm of word formation: depth no longer maintains its defined spatial character, but acquires more widely significant, barely measurable shapes. Instead of a linear configuration, we might see a pond, a lake, a sea—a body of water with a shimmering surface and hidden depths. Not engaged in measuring, we now see the sea, for instance, with but a rudimentary differentiation between the experience and the water before us. By the same token, our sense of self at this moment is not separated categorically from the element outside. We see and can be seen—in this intertwinement, the world is on the verge of speaking to us, and will do so once we stop babbling and begin to listen. A fish, a frog, a creature never seen before may rise from the depths and address our woes in what later might be categorized as a merely hallucinatory event.

Being in the realm of an early idiom, then, would be associated with uniquely alive, wondrous spheres where we speak and are spoken in ever-shifting configurations. What if, however, once upon a time we were spoken relentlessly? Or if we saw and desired, but our eyes and wishes were not met in turn? What if we then spoke and acted from the fury of a neglected, ridiculed, appropriated existence?

In the Beginning

Underneath the plots and the interpretations, stories of anger wait to be heard along with those of wonder.

Whenever the dominant language begins to recede, a certain fluidity appears: a sequence of assertions crumbles; something does not make sense; an ambivalence derails the tale's progression; a counter-statement lurks in a self-assured phrase. Apperceiving, D. W. Winnicott tells us in his preoedipal narrative,[6] involves one's own seeing before it has hardened into objective coinage. In apperceiving we are close to the creative moment, which does not apprehend what is believed to be there, but touches upon a fresh reality not yet shared by a larger community.[7] Narcissus appears in loving delusions and affirmations, above the blissful and—with the apperceptive moment remaining tied to itself—abysmal water.

Language shines in such regions. Seen through the haze of retrospection, or measured against the organized, dressed-up body of adult pronouncement, early linguistic articulation appears to be a *Schein*, a seemingly real phenomenon. In its own sphere, however, this *Schein* radiates with an altogether present, and at times frightful immediacy. There and then, early times come alive: their promises, their disenchantments, and their horrors.

2
Brüder Grimm
Der König vom goldenen Berg[8]

*E*in *Kaufmann, der hatte zwei Kinder, einen Buben und ein Mädchen, die waren beide noch klein und konnten noch nicht laufen. Es giengen aber zwei reichbeladene Schiffe von ihm auf dem Meer, und sein ganzes Vermögen war darin, und wie er meinte dadurch viel Geld zu gewinnen, kam die Nachricht, sie wären versunken. Da war er nun statt eines reichen Mannes ein armer Mann und hatte nichts mehr übrig als einen Acker vor der Stadt. Um sich sein Unglück ein wenig aus den Gedanken zu schlagen, gieng er hinaus auf den Acker, und wie er da so auf- und abging, stand auf einmal ein kleines schwarzes Männchen neben ihm und fragte warum er so traurig wäre, und was er sich so sehr zu Herzen nähme. Da sprach der Kaufmann 'wenn du mir helfen könntest, wollt ich dir es wohl sagen.' 'Wer weiß,' antwortete das schwarze Männchen, 'vielleicht helf ich dir.' Da erzählte der Kaufmann daß ihm sein ganzer Reichthum auf dem Meer zu Grunde gegangen wäre, und hätte er nichts mehr übrig als diesen Acker.' 'Bekümmere dich nicht,' sagte das Männchen, 'wenn du mir versprichst das, was dir zu Haus am ersten widers Bein stößt, in zwölf Jahren hierher auf den Platz zu bringen, sollst du Geld haben so viel du willst.' Der Kaufmann dachte 'was kann das anders sein als mein Hund?' aber an seinen kleinen Jungen dachte er nicht und sagte ja, gab dem schwarzen Mann Handschrift und Siegel darüber und gieng nach Haus.*

Als er nach Haus kam, da freute sich sein kleiner Junge so sehr darüber, daß er sich an den Bänken hielt, zu ihm herbei wackelte und ihn an den Beinen fest packte. Da erschrack der Vater, denn es fiel ihm sein Versprechen ein und er wußte nun was er verschrieben hatte: weil er aber immer noch kein Geld in seinen Kisten und Kasten fand, dachte er es wäre nur ein Spaß von dem Männchen gewesen. Einen Monat nachher gieng er auf den Boden und wollte altes Zinn zusammen suchen und verkaufen, da sah er einen großen Haufen Geld liegen. Nun war er wieder guter Dinge, kaufte ein, ward

The King of the Golden Mountain

A merchant had two children, a boy and a girl: both were still little and not yet able to walk. Now, it so happened that two of his richly laden ships were crossing the ocean, containing his entire fortune, and just as he was thinking that he could make lots of money with them, news arrived that they had sunk. So now, instead of a rich man, he was a poor one and had nothing left but a field outside the town. In order to take his mind off his trouble for a while, he went out to this field, and as he was walking back and forth there, a little black man suddenly stood by his side and asked why he was so sad and what he was taking to heart so much. And the merchant spoke: "If you could help me, I would gladly tell you." "Who knows," replied the little black man, "perhaps I will help you." So then the merchant told him that his entire fortune had sunk at sea and that he had nothing left but this field. "Do not worry," said the little man, "if you promise me that in twelve years you will bring to this same place whatever first brushes against your leg when you return home, you shall have all the money you want." The merchant thought: "What else could that be but my dog?" And he did not think of his little boy and said yes, gave the black man his written and sealed promise, and went home.

When he got home, there he was, his little boy who was so happy to see him that, holding on to some benches, he toddled over to him and clasped him by the legs. At that the father was frightened, for he remembered his promise, and now he knew what he had signed away; but because he still found no money in his coffers and boxes, he thought the little man had just been joking. One month later he went up to the attic to look for old tinware to sell; and there he saw a big pile of money. Now he was in a good mood again, purchased new wares, became a greater merchant than before, and thought that everything was just fine. Meanwhile the boy grew tall, and at the same time smart and clever. Yet the more the end of the twelve years approached, the

ein größerer Kaufmann als vorher und ließ Gott einen guten Mann sein. Unterdessen ward der Junge groß und dabei klug und gescheidt. Je näher aber die zwölf Jahre herbei kamen, je sorgvoller ward der Kaufmann, so daß man ihm die Angst im Gesicht sehen konnte. Da fragte ihn der Sohn einmal was ihm fehlte: der Vater wollte es nicht sagen, aber jener hielt so lange an, bis er ihm endlich sagte er hätte ihn, ohne zu wissen was er verspräche, einem schwarzen Männchen zugesagt und vieles Geld dafür bekommen. Er hätte seine Handschrift mit Siegel darüber gegeben, und nun müßte er ihn, wenn zwölf Jahre herum wären, ausliefern. Da sprach der Sohn 'o Vater, laßt euch nicht bang sein, das soll schon gut werden, der Schwarze hat keine Macht über mich.'

Der Sohn ließ sich von dem Geistlichen segnen, und als die Stunde kam, giengen sie zusammen hinaus auf den Acker, und der Sohn machte einen Kreiß und stellte sich mit seinem Vater hinein. Da kam das schwarze Männchen und sprach zu dem Alten 'hast du mitgebracht, was du mir versprochen hast?' Er schwieg still, aber der Sohn fragte 'was willst du hier?' Da sagte das schwarze Männchen 'ich habe mit deinem Vater zu sprechen und nicht mit dir.' Der Sohn antwortete 'du hast meinen Vater betrogen und verführt, gib die Handschrift heraus.' 'Nein,' sagte das schwarze Männchen, 'mein Recht geb ich nicht auf.' Da redeten sie noch lange mit einander, endlich wurden sie einig, der Sohn, weil er nicht dem Erbfeind und nicht mehr seinem Vater zugehörte, sollte sich in ein Schiffchen setzen, das auf einem hinabwärts fließenden Wasser stände, und der Vater sollte es mit seinem eigenen Fuß fortstoßen, und dann sollte der Sohn dem Wasser überlassen bleiben. Da nahm er Abschied von seinem Vater, setzte sich in ein Schiffchen, und der Vater mußte es mit seinem eigenen Fuß fortstoßen. Das Schiffchen schlug um, so daß der unterste Theil oben war, die Decke aber im Wasser; und der Vater glaubte, sein Sohn wäre verloren, gieng heim und trauerte um ihn.

Das Schiffchen aber versank nicht, sondern floß ruhig fort, und der Jüngling saß sicher darin, und so floß es lange, bis es endlich an einem unbekannten Ufer festsitzen blieb. Da stieg er ans Land, sah ein schönes Schloß vor sich liegen und gieng darauf los. Wie er aber hineintrat, war es verwünscht: er gieng durch alle Zimmer, aber sie waren leer bis er in die letzte Kammer kam, da lag eine Schlange darin und ringelte sich. Die Schlange aber war eine verwünschte Jungfrau, die freute sich, wie sie ihn sah, und sprach zu ihm 'kommst du, mein Erlöser? auf dich habe ich schon zwölf Jahre

more worried grew the merchant, and his fear could be seen in his face. So one day the son asked him what was wrong; the father did not want to talk about it, but the son kept on asking until, finally, the father told him: how without knowing what he was promising he had pledged him to a little black man and received lots of money in return; how he had set his hand and seal to the promise; and how he now, once the twelve years had run their course, would have to hand him over. Then the son spoke: "My father, do not be afraid, things will be alright, the black fellow has no power over me."

The son had himself blessed by the priest, and when the hour came, he and his father went out to the field, and the son drew a circle and placed himself inside it with his father. Right then the little black man came and said to the old man: "Have you brought with you what you promised me?" The father remained silent, but the son asked: "What do you want here?" Whereupon the little black man said: "It is with your father that I wish to speak and not with you." The son answered: "You have betrayed and seduced my father, give back the contract." "No," said the little black man, "I will not give up my rights." Then they talked to each other for a long time; at last they agreed: because the son did not belong to the archenemy nor any longer to his father, he was to place himself in a little ship, which would lie upon a downward-flowing stream, and the father was to push it off with his own foot, and then the son was to be left to the waters. Thereupon he took leave of his father and sat down in a little ship, and the father had to push it off with his own foot. The little ship turned over so that the bottom was up, and the top in the water; and the father believed that his son was lost, went home and mourned for him.

Yet the little ship did not sink, but floated quietly away, and the youth sat safely inside, and thus it floated for a long time until in the end it came to rest at an unknown shore. Thereupon he stepped ashore, saw a beautiful castle lying before him, and set out for it. When he entered, however, it turned out to be under a spell; he went through all the rooms, but found them empty till he came to the last chamber where a snake lay writhing. The snake, however, was a spellbound maiden; she was happy to see him and said: "Are you here, my savior? For you I have already been waiting twelve years; this kingdom is under a spell, and you must save it." "How can I do that?" he asked. "Tonight twelve black men will come, covered with chains; they will ask you what you are doing here; but be silent then and give them no answer, and let them do what they will to you: they will torment you, beat and stab you—let

gewartet; dies Reich ist verwünscht, und du mußt es erlösen.' 'Wie kann ich das?' fragte er. 'Heute Nacht kommen zwölf schwarze Männer, die mit Ketten behangen sind, die werden dich fragen was du hier machst, da schweig aber still und gib ihnen keine Antwort, und laß sie mit dir machen was sie wollen: sie werden dich quälen, schlagen und stechen, laß alles geschehen, nur rede nicht; um zwölf Uhr müssen sie wieder fort. Und in der zweiten Nacht werden wieder zwölf andere kommen, in der dritten vier und zwanzig, die werden dir den Kopf abhauen: aber um zwölf Uhr ist ihre Macht vorbei, und wenn du dann ausgehalten und kein Wörtchen gesprochen hast, so bin ich erlöst. Ich komme zu dir, und habe in einer Flasche das Wasser des Lebens, damit bestreiche ich dich, und dann bist du wieder lebendig und gesund wie zuvor.' 'Da sprach er 'gerne will ich dich erlösen.' Es geschah nun alles so, wie sie gesagt hatte: die schwarzen Männer konnten ihm kein Wort abzwingen, und in der dritten Nacht ward die Schlange zu einer schönen Königstochter, die kam mit dem Wasser des Lebens und machte ihn wieder lebendig. Und dann fiel sie ihm um den Hals und küßte ihn, und war Jubel und Freude im ganzen Schloß. Da wurde ihre Hochzeit gehalten, und er war König vom g o l d e n e n B e r g e.

Also lebten sie vergnügt zusammen, und die Königin gebar einen schönen Knaben. Acht Jahre waren schon herum, da fiel ihm sein Vater ein und sein Herz ward bewegt, und er wünschte ihn einmal heimzusuchen. Die Königin wollte ihn aber nicht fortlassen und sagte 'ich weiß schon daß es mein Unglück ist,' er ließ ihr aber keine Ruhe bis sie einwilligte. Beim Abschied gab sie ihm noch einen Wünschring und sprach 'nimm diesen Ring und steck ihn an deinen Finger, so wirst du alsbald dahin versetzt, wo du dich hinwünschest, nur mußt du mir versprechen daß du ihn nicht gebrauchst, mich von hier weg zu deinem Vater zu wünschen.' Er versprach ihr das, steckte den Ring an seinen Finger und wünschte sich heim vor die Stadt, wo sein Vater lebte. Im Augenblick befand er sich auch dort und wollte in die Stadt: wie er aber vors Thor kam, wollten ihn die Schildwachen nicht einlassen, weil er seltsame und doch so reiche und prächtige Kleider an hatte. Da gieng er auf einen Berg, wo ein Schäfer hütete, tauschte mit diesem die Kleider und zog den alten Schäferrock an und gieng also ungestört in die Stadt ein. Als er zu seinem Vater kam, gab er sich zu erkennen, der aber glaubte nimmermehr daß es sein Sohn wäre und sagte er hätte zwar einen Sohn gehabt, der wäre aber längst todt: doch weil er sähe daß er ein armer dürftiger Schäfer wäre, so wollte er ihm einen Teller voll zu essen geben. Da

all of this happen, only do not speak; at twelve o'clock they must leave. And in the second night twelve others will come, in the third, twenty-four: these will chop off your head; but at twelve o'clock their power will be gone, and then, if you have endured it all and not spoken a single word, I shall be saved. I will come to you, and in a bottle I will have the Water of Life; with that I will rub you, and then you will be as alive and well as before." Thereupon he spoke: "I will be glad to save you." Now everything happened as she had said: the black men could not force one word out of him, and in the third night the snake turned into a beautiful king's daughter; and she came with the Water of Life and brought him back to life again. And then she threw her arms around him and kissed him, and there was jubilation and joy all over the castle. Then their wedding was celebrated, and he was King of the G o l- d e n M o u n t a i n.

Thus they lived together happily, and the queen gave birth to a beautiful boy. Eight years had already gone by when the king thought of his father, and his heart was moved, and he wished to visit him. The queen, however, did not want to let him go away and said: "I know beforehand that this will bring me misfortune." He, however, gave her no peace until she consented. Upon his departure, she gave him a wishing ring and said: "Take this ring and put it on your finger, and then, wherever you wish to be, thereto you will be moved; but you must promise me that you will not use it to wish me away from here to your father." He promised her that, put the ring on his finger, and wished he were home, outside the town where his father lived. In an instant he was there and set out for the town; but as he came to the gate, the sentries would not let him go in, because he wore such strange and yet such rich and magnificent clothes. So he climbed a hill where a shepherd was tending his flock, exchanged clothes with him and put on the shepherd's old coat, and thus passed into the town unquestioned. When he came to his father, he made himself known to him, but his father did not at all believe that this was his son and said that, true enough, he had had a son who, however, had been dead for a long time; but, seeing that he was a poor, shabby shepherd, he would give him a plate of food. Thereupon the shepherd said to his parents: "I am truly your son, do you not know a mark on my body whereby you could recognize me?" "Yes," said his mother, "our son had a raspberry mark under his right arm." He slipped back his shirt, and so they saw the raspberry mark under his right arm, and no longer doubted that this was their son. Then he told them that he was King of the Golden Mountain, and that a king's

sprach der Schäfer zu seinen Eltern 'ich bin wahrhaftig euer Sohn, wißt ihr kein Mal an meinem Leibe, woran ihr mich erkennen könnt?' 'Ja,' sagte die Mutter, 'unser Sohn hatte eine Himbeere unter dem rechten Arm.' Er streifte das Hemd zurück, da sahen sie die Himbeere unter seinem rechten Arm und zweifelten nicht mehr daß es ihr Sohn wäre. Darauf erzählte er ihnen er wäre König vom goldenen Berge und eine Königstochter wäre seine Gemahlin, und sie hätten einen schönen Sohn von sieben Jahren. Da sprach der Vater 'nun und nimmermehr ist das wahr: das ist mir ein schöner König, der in einem zerlumpten Schäferrock hergeht.' Da ward der Sohn zornig und drehte, ohne an sein Versprechen zu denken, den Ring herum und wünschte beide, seine Gemahlin und sein Kind, zu sich. In dem Augenblick waren sie auch da, aber die Königin, die klagte und weinte, und sagte er hätte sein Wort gebrochen und hätte sie unglücklich gemacht. Er sagte 'ich habe es unachtsam gethan und nicht mit bösem Willen und redete ihr zu; sie stellte sich auch als gäbe sie nach, aber sie hatte Böses im Sinn.

Da führte er sie hinaus vor die Stadt auf den Acker und zeigte ihr das Wasser, wo das Schiffchen war abgestoßen worden, und sprach dann 'ich bin müde, setze dich nieder, ich will ein wenig auf deinem Schooß schlafen.' Da legte er seinen Kopf auf ihren Schooß und sie lauste ihn ein wenig, bis er einschlief. Als er eingeschlafen war, zog sie erst den Ring von seinem Finger, dann zog sie den Fuß unter ihm weg und ließ nur den Toffel zurück: hierauf nahm sie ihr Kind in den Arm und wünschte sich wieder in ihr Königreich. Als er aufwachte, lag er da ganz verlassen, und seine Gemahlin und das Kind waren fort und der Ring vom Finger auch, nur der Toffel stand noch da zum Wahrzeichen. 'Nach Haus zu deinen Eltern kannst du nicht wieder gehen,' dachte er, 'die würden sagen, du wärst ein Hexenmeister, du willst aufpacken und gehen bis du in dein Königreich kommst.' Also gieng er fort und kam endlich zu einem Berg, vor dem drei Riesen standen und mit einander stritten, weil sie nicht wußten wie sie ihres Vaters Erbe theilen sollten. Als sie ihn vorbei gehen sahen, riefen sie ihn an und sagten kleine Menschen hätten klugen Sinn, er sollte ihnen die Erbschaft vertheilen. Die Erbschaft aber bestand aus einem Degen, wenn einer den in die Hand nahm und sprach 'Köpf alle runter, nur meiner nicht,' so lagen alle Köpfe auf der Erde: zweitens aus einem Mantel, wer den anzog, war unsichtbar; drittens aus ein paar Stiefeln, wenn man die angezogen hatte und sich wohin wünschte, so war man im Augenblick da. Er sagte 'gebt mir die drei Stücke damit ich probieren könnte ob sie noch in gutem Stande sind.' Da gaben sie

The King of the Golden Mountain

daughter was his wife, and that they had a beautiful, seven-year-old son. And the father said: "Never can that be true: that is a fine king indeed who walks about in a ragged shepherd's coat." At that the son became angry and, without thinking of his promise, turned around the ring and wished both his wife and his child were with him. And in an instant they were there, but the queen lamented and wept, and said he had broken his word and had made her unhappy. He said: "I did it without thinking and not out of ill will," and tried to cheer her up; and she pretended to give in, but she had evil on her mind.

Thereupon he led her out of the town to the field and showed her the water where the little ship had been pushed off, and then he said: "I am tired, sit down, I want to sleep a bit on your lap." And he laid his head on her lap, and she loused him a bit until he fell asleep. When he had fallen asleep, she first pulled the ring off his finger; then she pulled her foot out from under him and left only her slipper behind; and then she took her child in her arms and wished herself back in her kingdom. When he awoke, he was lying there all alone, and his wife and child were gone, and so was the ring from his finger; only the slipper was still there as a token. "You cannot go home to your parents again," he thought, "they would say you are a warlock. So you must pack and walk, until you reach your kingdom." Thus he went away and finally came to a mountain before which three giants stood who were quarreling with each other, because they did not know how to divide their father's inheritance. When they saw him passing by, they called out to him and said small people were smart, and that he should distribute their inheritance for them. Now, the inheritance consisted, first, of a sword: if you took that into your hand and said: "All heads off, but not mine," instantly all heads would lie on the ground; second, of a cloak that, if you put that on, would make you invisible; and third, of a pair of boots that, once you had put those on and had wished yourself somewhere, would get you there in an instant. He said: "Give me these three things so that I may test if they still are in good condition." So they gave him the cloak, and when he had put it on, he was invisible and had changed into a fly. Then he took his own form again and said: "The cloak is good, now give me the sword." They said: "No, that we will not give you! If you said: 'All heads off, but not mine,' all our heads would be off, and you alone would still have yours." Yet they gave it to him on condition that he would try it out on a tree. This he did, and the sword cut a tree trunk in two as if it were a straw. Now he wanted to have the boots,

ihm den Mantel, und als er ihn umgehängt hatte, war er unsichtbar und war in eine Fliege verwandelt. Dann nahm er wieder seine Gestalt an und sprach 'der Mantel ist gut, 'nun gebt mir das Schwert.' Sie sagten 'nein, das geben wir nicht! wenn du sprächst "Köpf alle runter, nur meiner nicht!" so wären unsere Köpfe alle herab und du allein hättest den deinigen noch.' Doch gaben sie es ihm unter der Bedingung daß ers an einem Baum probieren sollte. Das that er und das Schwert zerschnitt den Stamm eines Baums wie einen Strohhalm. Nun wollt er noch die Stiefeln haben, sie sprachen aber 'nein, die geben wir nicht weg, wenn du sie angezogen hättest und wünschtest dich oben auf den Berg, so stünden wir da unten und hätten nichts.' 'Nein,' sprach er, 'das will ich nicht thun.' Da gaben sie ihm auch die Stiefeln. Wie er nun alle drei Stücke hatte, so dachte er an nichts als an seine Frau und sein Kind und sprach so vor sich hin 'ach wäre ich auf dem goldenen Berg,' und alsbald verschwand er vor den Augen der Riesen, und war also ihr Erbe getheilt. Als er nah beim Schloß war, hörte er Freudengeschrei, Geigen und Flöten, und die Leute sagten ihm seine Gemahlin feierte ihre Hochzeit mit einem andern. Da ward er zornig und sprach 'die Falsche, sie hat mich betrogen und mich verlassen, als ich eingeschlafen war.' Da hieng er seinen Mantel und gieng unsichtbar ins Schloß hinein. Als er in den Saal eintrat, war da eine große Tafel mit köstlichen Speisen besetzt, und die Gäste aßen und tranken, lachten und scherzten. Sie aber saß in der Mitte in prächtigen Kleidern auf einem königlichen Sessel und hatte die Krone auf dem Haupt. Er stellte sich hinter sie und niemand sah ihn. Wenn sie ihr ein Stück Fleisch auf den Teller legten, nahm er ihn weg und aß es: und wenn sie ihr ein Glas Wein einschenkten, nahm ers weg und tranks aus; sie gaben ihr immer, und sie hatte doch immer nichts, denn Teller und Glas verschwanden augenblicklich. Da ward sie bestürzt und schämte sie sich, stand auf und gieng in ihre Kammer und weinte, er aber gieng hinter ihr her. Da sprach sie 'ist denn der Teufel über mir, oder kam mein Erlöser nie?' Da schlug er ihr ins Angesicht und sagte 'kam dein Erlöser nie? er ist über dir, du Betrügerin. Habe ich das an dir verdient?' Da machte er sich sichtbar, gieng in den Saal und rief 'die Hochzeit ist aus, der wahre König ist gekommen!' Die Könige, Fürsten und Räthe, die da versammelt waren, höhnten und verlachten ihn: er aber gab kurze Worte und sprach 'wollt ihr hinaus oder nicht?' Da wollten sie ihn fangen und drangen auf ihn ein, aber er zog sein Schwert und sprach 'Köpf alle runter, nur meiner nicht.' Da rollten alle Köpfe zur Erde, und er war allein der Herr und war wieder König vom goldenen Berge.[9]

but they said: "No, those we will not give away; if you'd put them on and wished yourself up on the mountain, we'd stand down here with nothing." "No," he said, "I would not do that." So they gave him the boots as well. Now that he had all three things, he thought of nothing but his wife and child, and he talked to himself as follows: "Ah, if only I were on the Golden Mountain"; and instantly he disappeared from the sight of the giants, and thus their inheritance was divided. When he was near his castle, he heard shouts of joy, and violins, and flutes, and the people told him that his wife was celebrating her wedding with someone else. Thereupon he turned angry and uttered: "That false woman, she betrayed me and left me when I had fallen asleep." Then he put on his cloak and, now invisible, went into the castle. When he entered the hall, there was a large table covered with exquisite food, and the guests were eating and drinking, laughing and joking. And she sat in the middle in a royal chair in splendid garments, with her crown upon her head. He placed himself behind her, and no one saw him. When they put a piece of meat on her plate, he took the plate away and ate the meat; and when they poured her a glass of wine, he took it away and drank it; they gave her more and more, and yet she never got anything, for plate and glass vanished instantly. Now she felt embarrassed and ashamed, arose and went to her chamber and wept, and he followed her. Then she said: "Am I in the devil's grip, or did my savior never come?" At that he struck her in the face, and said: "Did your savior never come? He has you in his grip, you cheat. Have I deserved this from you?" Now he made himself visible, went into the hall, and shouted: "The wedding is over, the true king has come!" The kings, princes, and councilors who were assembled there jeered and laughed at him; and he uttered curt words and said: "Will you get out of here, or not?" Now they tried to catch him, and they closed in on him, but he drew his sword and spoke: "All heads off, but not mine." At that all heads rolled to the ground, and he alone was master, and once again King of the Golden Mountain.[10]

3

A Yearning at the Heart of Terror: Language and Psyche in "The King of the Golden Mountain"

> Sometimes I ask myself whether it will ever be possible for us to grasp the extent of the loneliness and desertion to which we were exposed as children...
>
> ALICE MILLER
> *Das Drama des begabten Kindes*

"The King of the Golden Mountain" in the Grimms' collection of fairy tales offers a compelling plot in which the protagonist turns into a monster who speaks and enacts the words: "All heads off, but not mine" (11). In the multivalent language of the text, however, a story underneath and around the plot takes place as well. In that story, early linguistic and psychic events occur with extraordinary immediacy—before our eyes and in the modulations at play in our ears. Such perceptions indeed require a willingness to let the narrative be at play in its subversive suggestions and revelations. Away from the plot, and yet intricately intertwined with its statements and its relentless progression, a variant story of rage and torment envelops readers young and old in a subliminal fashion.[11] Buried events and sensibilities resonate in a language that time and again resists translation into preorganized forms of communication. A merchant subjects his son to unspeakable treatment: at its heart, this story falls silent. In doing so, it emits signals that indicate a relationship between language and oppression: in the words and images presented to us as fairy tale, a terror reverberates, but does not unfold in syntactical threads—narrative cohesion disintegrates. The sights and sounds that then press through the linguistic veneer, defy rational, let alone interpretive containment. An idiom of experience punctures the tale's surface: memory comes alive.

Rage and Splitting

At first sight, the tale proceeds with brutal directness.[12] Words explode with primary force, turning into action at the very moment at which they are spoken: "'All heads off, but not mine.' At that all heads rolled..." From the king's perspective, this is how he defends himself. Everybody "closed in on him"; now he can breathe freely. Everyone "jeered and laughed at him"; now there is peace and quiet. In the midst of an exuberant, noisy crowd, his wife had been sitting "in a royal chair" (13) at her wedding to another man. Now all chairs are his. What happened to his son of whom he had thought on his way back to the Golden Mountain? That is the last we hear of his offspring.

At the end of the tale, the king's rage comes to a halt. He now does not rush forward in anger, intent on annihilating whomever crosses his path. He is somewhere where he was before, repeating something he knows from times past. This is a fairy-tale moment at which "once again" (13) he is King of the Golden Mountain. It is a moment of ultimate power. The time that was is present once again and might be so forever. Who could be there to challenge the ruler? He might create his own calendar, counting the years from now on forward in his kingdom. In being now where he was then and might well be in times to come, the king resides in a singularity in which the world appears to be under control once and for all—he "alone" its "master" (13). Is this supreme moment that of a murderer, dictator, or creator? "The King of the Golden Mountain" takes us to a realm where such possibilities dwell side by side. How exactly are these disturbing proximities configured, and how do they come about in the course of the text? How can we communicate about a matter that in its ambiguity undermines the language in which we make ourselves understood by making distinctions?

The king's wife experiences the tale's harshness first-hand. As she arrives at the threshold of a new life—with her former husband seemingly gone for good—events take a curious and humiliating turn. She is about to enjoy her wedding meal, but her plate and glass vanish the moment she is being served. Distressed and embarrassed, she retreats into her chamber, tears flowing down her face. In her despair, she utters to herself: "Am I in the devil's grip, or did my savior never come?" (13). About to be married to the new ruler, the former king's wife feels belittled and helpless as a child might when reaching out for food in vain. Faced with her calamity, the queen begins to perceive her world in terms of highly pronounced manifestations of good and evil. The "devil" and the "savior" mark opposite ends of a wide spectrum. The queen in her distraught condition is taken to borderline zones[13] where good and evil are "split"[14] and experienced in rapid oscillation, never settling into a middle ground where they might coexist in various ways.

In her chamber, the queen moves back toward the spheres of early childhood where delight and despair hardly connected with each other. We barely remember such times. Things then, it appears, were either good or bad, or rather there were no stable things to speak of beyond the all-powerful care one relied on for better or for worse.[15] At first sight, the wedding scene seems to belong to a later period in the queen's lifetime. Yet it forces her back toward her all but forgotten husband in a trajectory of submission, in which the wedding vows take on an ominously primordial meaning. As she celebrates her new union, the reappearing husband is not only about to claim her once again as his wife, but pushes her back toward much earlier times. In referring to the devil and "my savior," the queen comes close to perceiving the evil one as "über mir" (12), "above me." As she loses her bearings, she finds herself on the brink of disintegration.

The child we begin to glimpse in the queen is of the early age in which splitting under the sway of a powerful parental authority is a way of life and a source of potential annihilation. Then as now, she cannot control her food as it vanishes before her very eyes. As the words about the devil and the savior cross her lips, the still invisible king, in an outburst of anger, hits her in the face. "Did your savior never come?" asks the angry phantom, asserting that he "has you in his grip" (13)—more closely translated: "He is above you." At the mercy of her tormentor, this child is all but deprived of the possibility of responding in terms of her own self, precarious as it is to begin with in the childhood to which she has regressed. Made to carry the guilt for events she was forced to suffer, she is further assailed for being a "cheat," and placed before the former king who makes "himself visible" (13). He appears when she is hardly able to situate him in a reality outside of herself. What she sees might be a figment of her imagination. In the remainder of the tale we do not hear of her again.

The man's boundless rage takes over. As all heads roll onto the ground, the tale reaches its sinister ending. A madman goes about his business. No one is there to populate the territory this "true king" (13), as he calls himself, has just reclaimed. The scene is a familiar one. While the king's own family is disappearing, his childhood looms large in and around the formulations at the end. A king speaks and draws his sword, but so does the little boy in him who ventures out into a world that either will be his entirely or, should his childhood terrors return, will not respond to him at all. His language, reminiscent of creative, psychotically tinged utterances,[16] asserts itself beyond all bounds, but it might fail at any moment. The boy in the king is not sure of himself. He needs to be spectacularly powerful in order to experience himself as the master of things and people. It is a self-canceling experience in which at the height of achievement he stands alone.

His words are "curt" (13). They fulfill their function immediately—all heads roll instantly—and they pose mercilessly oppositional alternatives: "Will you get out of here, or not?" (13), he exclaims just before everyone is cut down by his sword. Uttered on the verge of action, such words are magically active beyond their linguistic confines. In their intense manifestations, early words are both powerful and subjectively charged.[17] Freshly launched, the toddler's pronouncements stand out to be seen and heard, as does the king.

Divergent Languages

Who is the little boy who speaks and acts through the king? Why does the latter's closeness to the experience of early linguistic engagement take on a deadly dimension? Why is there an excess of self-assertion that does not allow others to survive the outburst? What characterized the familial environment in which this particular boy first learned to speak? The merchant at the beginning of "The King of the Golden Mountain" has two little children, a boy and a girl. Both are "not yet able to walk" (5). More importantly to him, it seems, the merchant possesses two richly laden ships. These vessels, in curious juxtaposition with his children, were crossing the sea, "giengen" (4) —"walked"—on the ocean. In their linguistic configuration, the ships perform a movement that still eludes the children. The money to be made during their journey occupies the tale's foreground, and the merchant's mind: he "was thinking" (5) that he was about to profit greatly. We do not hear of his feelings. When news arrives that the ships have sunk, the merchant tries to take his "mind" (5) off his misfortune.

Throughout this dramatically condensed beginning, walking figures prominently. If we are as alert to particular words as toddlers who are learning to speak at about the time at which they begin to walk, a richly modulated sequence unfolds. The children who could not "walk" are immediately followed by the ships that, literally translated, "walked," "giengen," and soon thereafter by the merchant who walked, "gieng," to his field in order to gain some respite from his misfortune, and who on that field went back and forth, "auf- und abging" (4). The story, in which the children who cannot yet walk are relegated to a background vis-à-vis the commercial and adult subject of the ships, nevertheless continues in the verbalizations of walking, and furthermore with a little man who suddenly "stood" (5) next to the merchant. At that point, the theme of language enters more visibly into the tale. The news of the calamity at sea had implied a linguistic communication. Now such communication turns more explicit. Once the little man has asked the merchant to remark on his sadness, a series of references to speaking and telling follows.

When the little man first appears in the tale, his language is concerned with feeling, with the "heart" (5). He stands in the field, brings the merchant's walking to a halt, and initiates a momentous dialogue. The two men enter into a contract that will forever affect the little boy. At the same time, the narrative is beginning to develop in its linguistic richness and complexity. From the start, "The King of the Golden Mountain" reflects a sensibility for literal and immediate linguistic expression. Vistas onto a childhood universe open up as we respond to the various verbal actualizations, the different stories under the narrative veneer.

Although the little man inquires about the merchant's feeling, the latter holds on to his cognitive and commercial orientation. He defines the help he has in mind in terms of his lost riches, and emphasizes that he has nothing left but his field. The text, meanwhile, hints at crucial implications of the merchant's pronouncements. All of his wealth, he relates, has—literally—"gone" ("gegangen," 4) under at sea. Once again the movement of walking resonates in the narrative, but the merchant does not connect with the concomitant story of early childhood.

From its beginning, "The King of the Golden Mountain" suggests different styles[18] of linguistic communication. Responding to the little man in his unidirectional manner, the merchant "narrated," "erzählte" (4), of his commercial loss, whereas the man "said," "sagte" (4), that he should not worry. "Narrating" at this moment involves a plot-oriented activity in which goals, achievements, and clearly identifiable events are most important. In contradistinction to such a linear process, the little man's act of "saying" or "speaking" is not synonymous with expressing something in particular. Receiving "The King of the Golden Mountain" from the firmly defined grounds of an adult linguistic universe misses as well as subjugates the text's underlying drama and vitality. Although cast in negative terms, the little man speaks in a manner akin to experiential understandings of language in early childhood. Speaking multivalently, he at the same time enacts a communicative flexibility that reflects the experience of being a child in the process of learning and handling a language. Such speech precariously unfolds at the threshold between a world of many meanings, feelings, perceptions, and a more focused reality where much that does not fit a specific pursuit is shut out. "The King of the Golden Mountain" takes place on both sides of the threshold. Although this text charts a journey from early childhood forward, it also initiates a movement toward the buried sensibilities of the early years.

"'Do not worry,' said the little man, 'if you promise me'"—"wenn du mir versprichst" (4)—"'that in twelve years you will bring to this same place whatever first brushes against your leg when you return home, you shall have all the money you want'" (5). On the level of the plot, this promise is delineated clearly enough. The deal is defined as to time, place, and specific event. To this deal the merchant agrees after having clarified his thinking: "The merchant thought: 'What else could that be but my dog?'" The little man is attuned to his counterpart's emphasis on a willful suppression of feelings. When the merchant had first arrived on the field, he had tried, literally translated, to "beat his misfortune out of his thoughts for a while," "sich sein Unglück ein wenig aus den Gedanken zu schlagen" (4). The little man engages this mode by speaking of that which brushes, or rather "stößt" (4), "pushes," against the merchant's leg.

In the other, nonlinear story,[19] the "versprichst" (4) is much less certain than in the light of the deal. Like the modulations of *Gehen*, the promise recalls a time in which meanings and activities are not yet stabilized, but leave room for a multitude of perceptions as well as for trial and error. Listeners and readers sensitized to this wider context will perceive the possibility of a mistake in the promise, *Versprechen*, which also means "speaking in error." The story to which this error contributes might allow for a way out of the narrowly defined deal. If an error was indeed spoken, then there might be some leeway for reinterpreting a contract that turns out to be a fateful misunderstanding. On yet another level, the "versprichst" comprises a subtle warning for the merchant: is there something in the contract that involves an error?

The merchant, however, continues to deal on the level of thinking; he does "not think" (5) of the little boy. The little man receives the contract, signed and sealed by the merchant, who thus commits himself to a form of language decisively apart from the experience of speaking. Coming home, he enters into an experiential world nonetheless: there is his little boy, the toddler, holding on to benches on his way to him, finally clutching his father's legs in an embrace that spells his expulsion from the family. The father is not "horrified," as Manheim's translation has it (321). He merely "erschrack" (4), "was frightened," and quickly returns to his mental ways. Remembering his promise, "Versprechen," he "knew what he had signed away," "verschrieben" (4). Nothing happens for the moment; notwithstanding the presence of *Versprechen* and *Verschreiben*, with their potential implications of error, the merchant puts his faith in thinking—he "thought the little man had just been joking" (5).

Yet we hear another story when the little man speaks, and we feel it when we view the events from the little boy's perspective. Children, hearing and demanding to hear such a story time and again, know and feel the answers to these questions. In hearing what happens above, below, and around the established fairy-tale words and sentences, they approach a vocabulary. Adults, in turn, have a chance to become newly aware of the narrative's gripping strength. Hearing and telling the other story revives the memory of how it was when much, if not everything, depended on the big tall people: the little man of the field does not stand high above a child's world.

Submerged Complicity

When the boy is finally told what transpired on that field nearly twelve years ago, he is not scared, in spite of the frightful revelation. He feels he can communicate with the little man. He also feels that he can protect his father, and he speaks of the way his father might feel. The tale's familial hierarchy is reversed at this point. The merchant who had mainly "thought" about his son—although toward the end of the twelve years he had begun to feel "Angst" (6)—now hears his child speak to him: "My father, do not be afraid, things will be alright…" (7). In the dealings that follow, the father stands aside.

Yet the narrative does not proceed in a dualistic fashion. Just as the little man speaks with a childlike sensibility, but does not care for children, the son and the father possess languages and orientations that are not entirely opposed. The son, though victimized by his father, takes his side to some extent. He is a victim, yet keeps insight into his own situation at bay. He remains the child who cannot afford to fully see what has been happening to him. The two realms of the narrative thus interact rather than clash with each other.

Much of the hidden drama in "The King of the Golden Mountain" revolves around the son's complicity in his own victimization. As the twelfth year arrives, son and father go to the field where the contract was made. Starting out with the magical antidote to the line that relentlessly progresses toward a goal, the son produces a circle for his father and himself to stand in together. When the little man appears, the father does not respond to his question. The son does, speaking his own language and that of the father. "Have you brought with you what you promised me?" (7), the little man begins the exchange. Treating the son as a kind of thing, a "what," he revives the terms of the deal. With the word "promised," "versprochen" (6), however, the contract's complexity reappears. The son tries to shift the emphasis away from the deal, toward the little man's motivation: "What do you want here?" he asks, for a moment rising to the occasion. Rather than staying within the situation that designates him as a victim, he inquires into the agenda of one of his victimizers and into the nature of the place where he finds himself. Not willing to respond to the question, however, the little man instead attempts to initiate a dialogue with his fellow victimizer, the father: "It is with your father that I wish to speak"—"sprechen" (6)—"and not with you" (7), he rebuffs the son.

At this point the son steps back into the cycle of victimization. He does not insist on the revelation of the little man's motivation, but sides with his father. The language of confusion resurfaces as the son's own when he replies: "You have betrayed and seduced"—"verführt"—"my father, give back the contract." The exchange has come full circle from the initial "versprichst" (4) via the son's attempt at clarification and the little man's countermove of establishing a direct line to the father with "sprechen" (6): in "verführt" (6) the initial "Versprechen" (4) resonates.

The son's sensibility and forgiveness—for his father he partakes in the risks and the promises of linguistic multivalence—do not engender a response. The written contract, "Handschrift" (4), remains in place. At the end of the negotiations, the son more than ever is the object of the deal. He is put into a boat and kicked into a river by his father who, seeing the vessel capsize, believes that his offspring is on the way to his death. What could have been the son's liberation is turned upside down; the paternal dynamics of oppression and submission gain dominance.

Reemergence: A Language of Experience

Against all odds, the son survives the journey. A story emerges that has the trappings of good fortune. At "an unknown shore" (7), a new sense of time sets in. There is a change of pace, which is largely missed in Manheim's translation where the boat "floated gently down the river" (322); the clause, "and thus it floated for a long time" (7), is omitted in its entirety. This translational acceleration of time combines with spatial and linguistic changes in ways that create a tighter, more organized tale. Manheim's rendering of "Ufer" as "place" reflects a decrease of fluidity. The double omission of sitting further domesticizes the boat's journey: the young man—no longer is he referred to as "son"—finds himself inside the boat without a particular posture, and at its enigmatic destination the boat "stopped" (Manheim 322), a less descriptive formulation than "festsitzen blieb" (6), "remained sitting." *Sitzen* reactivates the toddler's dramatic history. In the capsized boat, the young man subsists "safely" (7), surrounded by fluid, as in a womb. He is on his way toward the time when he will emerge from his encasement and finally begin to walk: "Thereupon he stepped ashore," we read immediately after the boat "remained sitting," "stuck."

The young man who moves from sitting to climbing reminds us of his uncertain steps which had led him to a father who, towering high above him, had dealt him away. Growing up, in this context, literally means trying to ascend to higher places. The sense of achievement a toddler experiences when the world is opening up and magnificent things appear within reach, is diminished in Manheim's translation, which once again takes a somewhat impatient, adult view: "The boy went ashore and soon came to a magnificent castle, but when he went in, he saw it was bewitched" (322). In this version, the boy's movement toward and into the castle undergoes a radical abbreviation. The text had read: "Thereupon he stepped ashore, saw a beautiful castle lying before him, and set out for it. When he entered, however, it turned out to be under a spell…" ("Da stieg er ans Land, sah ein schönes Schloß vor sich liegen und gieng darauf los. Wie er aber hineintrat, war es verwünscht…" [6]). These words evoke a richly imaginative experience. "Schloß" phonetically resonates with "schönes" and "stieg," and similarly "sah" and "sich" add to the enchanted flow. In this way, too, the subliminal story, which draws on a multivalent and experientially vibrant language, remains alive.

Versprechen in its various meanings, whose simultaneous occurrence destabilizes the plot, lives on in *Verwünschen*, which at first sight denotes an act of sorcery, but also invokes the dynamics of *Wunsch*, "wish," "desire." Being bewitched carries with it an undertone of yearning. As the narrative continues, we are approaching the heart of the story of the young man who, having been severely mistreated in the course of the tale, is nearing a land of his own: "He went from room to room, and they were all empty except for the last, and there he saw a coiled snake. The snake was a bewitched maiden" (Manheim 322). In this translation, the plot progresses logically, step by step, up to the point where we are provided with the snake's identity. More closely rendered, the passage reads: He "went through all the rooms, but found them empty till he came to the last chamber where a snake lay writhing. The snake, however, was a spellbound maiden…" (7).

Taking place within the perimeters of *Verwünschen*, this explorative movement touches upon the biblical snake's lure. Rather than progressing from one space to the next, the protagonist traverses the rooms in their entirety. In this encompassing process, the last room forms a significantly different kind of enclosure; it is a "chamber," "Kammer" (6). In this particular place, the young man does not simply see a snake in its factual presence, but a powerfully suggestive animal that both occupies its special spot, lying there, and at the same time performs its twists and turns. Once again the "aber," not merely an oppositional "but," appears, contributing to the snake's ("Schlange aber," 6) mythological resonance.

Much is communicated, then, in the language of the text: the life of the underlying story depends on perceptions of variant, experiential elements in the plot's ostensible progression. Snakelike, the hidden story develops in twists and turns, occasionally turning back in on itself to start anew.

For twelve years, the snake has waited for her release. Twelve years have passed for the young man as well since his father dealt him away. Again at the edge of walking, and beginning to explore the world on his own two feet now, this resilient figure meets a young woman who herself wishes to step into life. In her condition, however, she does not possess feet. She has spent her life in the state from which the protagonist rises early in the tale when he hugs his father's legs. The young man, now experiencing reality with newly open eyes, meets his counterpart here. She greets him with the same feeling of joy, *Freude*, with which the toddler had once welcomed his father: she "freute sich" (6), "was happy," echoing the very words of the former occasion (4).

In the realm of the toddler and of early language experience, words are not yet amply available, nor are they tied to elaborate syntactic structures. More richly endowed with experiential properties than their adult successors, they are emotionally evocative. The snake's first utterance occurs in two simple words—"kommst du" (6), "are you here"—in a present tense that reverberates with her past life. And rather than forming a sentence that might meet expectations by beginning with the subject, as most translations do,[20] she more emotionally places "for you" at the forefront of her invocation of long years of waiting. She also reiterates "verwünscht" (8) with its echoes of promise, error, and desire: *Versprechen* and *Wunsch*. It is the third time that *Verwünschen* appears since the young man has climbed ashore. Spellbound, error-laden desire is about to take a course in which the number three—often indicative of a climactic sequence—figures prominently.[21]

A new beginning is under way for the protagonist, who at this early point encounters a young woman at the threshold of her own transformation. With the snake imagery in particular, mythical memory plays into this scene. At the same time, the narrative approaches its own, unstated beginnings. The boy's father, the merchant with the two children, is not said to have a wife. In discovering the "spellbound maiden" (7) in the castle, the protagonist makes contact with a feminine element that has been missing in the tale; although the protagonist's sister had appeared in its first sentence, she is not mentioned again.

In the language heard below the level of the plot through insistent repetitions and linguistic densities, knots are continually tied and untied. The father's promise, *Versprechen*, had exceeded his ability to control his dealings. Undercutting his awareness, this *Versprechen* had driven two, and more, stories at once, in which the narrative figures had been deeply entangled, with the exception of the little man. Once the *Verwünschen*, in which curse and desire interconnect enigmatically, has established its presence, both the *Verwünschen* and the *Versprechen* are drawn into a dynamics of salvation, *Erlösung*. Having been greeted as "Erlöser," "savior," the protagonist is told that he "must save," "erlösen" (8), the kingdom. *Lösen* includes "to loosen" in its semantic range. Age-old knots might unravel in the couple's new union. This exhilarating prospect, with its undertones of post-paradisiacal hopes of redemption, comes true, it seems, in an atmosphere of "jubilation" and, once again, "joy," "Freude" (8). The one who had been coldly *versprochen* and the other who had been *verwünscht* for twelve paralyzing years now step into their new life together, as King and Queen of the Golden Mountain. But do they?

Silence in the extreme is one of the conditions that had to be met before the new knot could be tied. The protagonist had to endure a series of terrifying tests without uttering a word. In itself, this does not seem to be at odds with the incipient story of love. The couple's encounter had come to pass in a sphere between language and silence, walking and crawling, dealing and feeling. This also had been the realm in which the narrative and the boy's misfortune had begun: setting out in his own way, he remains tied to his early experience. The young woman, furthermore, revives the memory of his forgotten sister with whom he had been on the verge of stepping into the world. In the snake, then, the boy also finds the one who belongs to his story to begin with.

A Time before Words

The narrative slides back and forth into and out of the realms from which it has been emerging: a time before words appears. Recalling the embryonic fluid, the "Water of Life" (9) brings the protagonist back into existence, after he has been beheaded in the ultimate test of his fearlessness. As forcefully as the "King of the Golden Mountain" speaks of the protagonist's journey back in life, and forward from death, the text is curiously devoid of his feelings. The rejoicing at the end of the torment occurs "all over the castle" (9); we do not hear of the young man's joy. His agony and reemergence fall short of transforming him into a freshly present being with his own narrative. As he enters into marriage, the young man still exhibits the marks of his father's deal and cruel kick. His silence when tortured connects with a familiar muteness: abandoned and abused, he has to some extent acquiesced in his ordeals. Although imbued with hope and suggestive of salvation, his underlying story remains abysmally complex.

After a good many years of living his new life, now possessing a son of his own, the king remembers his father. Again, his mother, who later turns out to be alive as well, is not mentioned. In terms of the explicit narrative, the king continues to affirm his paternal lineage in spite of his history. Yet a feminine underside of his story speaks in his desire, *Wunsch*, to visit his father: he wished—"wünschte"—to visit him, "ihn einmal heimzusuchen" (8). *Heimsuchen* also means "to devastate," while *Wunsch* resonates with the story of the snake. "Einmal," "once," furthermore resounds with times past and fairy-tale beginnings. The plot in which the king contemplates visiting his father barely overlies a story of deep memory, incipient rage, and ambivalent desire.

As throughout the narrative, the queen is somewhat aware of the underlying forces that spell misfortune and, in the end, catastrophe. She does not want her husband to go, but finally gives in to his insistence. Upon his departure, she provides him with a wishing ring. Not only is its shape reminiscent of the circle the protagonist had to leave behind on his way to the wedding, but the queen's words connect the ring with a whole range of earlier happenings and multivalent interactions. The ring will enable the king to be transported to a place of his choosing.

Such a linear trajectory, however, meets with immediate qualifications. The place would be one where "you wish to be," "du dich hinwünschest" (8). The *Wunsch* at this point recalls both the evil spell and the father's ill-conceived *Versprechen*. You "must promise"—"versprechen"—the queen demands as she lets go of the ring, "that you will not use it to wish me away from here to your father" (9). The king's agreement involves the fateful word: he "versprach" (8)—"promised"—to honor her wish.

The son does not wish to be inside of his father's town right away, although the ring gives him the power to do so. Rather the story underneath and around the plot asserts itself once again. It had been on a field outside of town where the child's father had first met the wily little man, and where it had been decided twelve years later that the son would be pushed into the stream. Now the son wishes himself to a spot "outside the town" (9), onto the terrain of the *Versprechen*. He returns to the realm where he had been abandoned twice before. There his story stands still. His silence in the midst of terror and forlornness remains present in speechless pain.

Desire and Catastrophe

In his "strange and yet...rich and magnificent" clothes, the son cannot gain entry into town. When he manages to pass the gate in a shepherd's coat, his father insists on judging him by his ragged appearance, proclaiming that his son has long since died. The latter calls upon his parents to identify him from a birthmark. Characteristically, the father remains unmoved. For the first and only time in the tale, the mother appears: "Yes," she says, "our son had a raspberry mark under his right arm" (9). Having been thus identified, the son speaks of his successful life. The father replies: "Never can that be true: that is a fine king indeed who walks about in a ragged shepherd's coat."

Treated like a deceitful child and rejected once again, the son is no longer able to compose himself. His rage, alive in the underlying story, overtakes him now. Propelled by his father's remark into the paternal world against which he rebels and to which he simultaneously succumbs in his rage, the son rapidly regresses to the time when he had been promised, *versprochen*, to the little man. Without thinking of his own *Versprechen*, he turns the wishing ring, and wishes—"wünschte" (10)—both his wife and his child to his father's house. The *Versprechen*, the ring in its wishing power and circularity, and the "wünschte"—in its proximity to *verwünschen, versprechen*, and *verführen*—reactivate the early, merciless story. The broken promise will push both husband and wife back toward the times of their bare survival.

Again the tale moves to the field before the town. As the protagonist sinks into sleep, with his head on his wife's lap, she takes the ring off his finger, pulls her foot out from under him, leaving only a slipper behind, and wishes herself and her child back to her own land. This surface plot is punctured by a word that brings with it the hidden story: "Toffel" (10)—"slipper" (11)—which echoes with "Teufel," "devil," and also recalls the little man who on this very site had proposed the contract with its Mephistophelian resonances.

At the end of his slumber, the king is alone, much as he had been before meeting the princess. Only "the slipper was still there as a token" (11), "Wahrzeichen" (10). The text before translation again reflects the story underneath the plot. In conjunction with "Toffel," it has "Wahrzeichen" (10), a "sign"—"Zeichen"—associated with "wahr," "true." More than a mere reminder of the absent wife, the "Toffel" speaks of the "truly" telling narrative, which now falls back toward its beginnings.

In its final phase, the tale offers a series of climactic events. Realizing that he cannot return to his parents, the son walks back toward his kingdom. At the foot of a mountain, he encounters three giants arguing over their inheritance: a sword that, if so asked, immediately takes off all heads; a cloak that renders its wearer invisible; and boots that instantly propel their owner wherever they are told to go. Asked to divide these items up for them, the protagonist demands to test each piece, thus bringing one after the other under his control. The final test, that of the boots, brings his trickery to a close and takes him back to the Golden Mountain, where he intrudes on his wife's wedding.

This plot, although rich in detail and colorful events, forms only a small part of the overall narrative. Intensely charged with the life the son never led, each of the inherited pieces recalls a painful past, and each of them will contribute to the cataclysmic future. The sword that upon command cuts off all heads points back to the protagonist's beheading. Then as now, his emotional response remains shrouded in silence. Yet his rage announces itself in the force with which he tests his sword, cutting a tree trunk in two as if it were made of straw.

The cloak that renders the protagonist invisible is reminiscent of the shepherd's garment that covered up his identity so that he could enter into his father's town. In order to be able to see his father, he had to appear to be someone he was not. The cloak recalls the early story in which the infant and toddler was not allowed to be himself. Now invisible in his human form, the cloaked protagonist metamorphoses into a fly.

With the pair of boots that expedites its owner to where he wishes to be, the story of the wishing ring takes a suggestive turn. Associated with the lovely and devilish significance of the "Toffel" (10)—"slipper"—his wife had left behind, these boots possess a near-fetishistic quality. The narrative, however, does not find containment in a fetishistically charged symbol. The returning king's fury is boundless, fed by a life story that now comes to a head.[22] In a present charged with the signs of the past, this man is gripped by anger beyond his control. Wrapped in the cloak that makes him invisible, he humiliates his wife and forces her into a disintegrative state close to his own. Dissonant themes of his life play out in the world around him, producing powerful effects. The heads that roll downward "to the ground" (13) follow the narrative's downward trajectory. The King of the Golden Mountain, whose own head had been severed from his body, now rules, disconnected, his very own story. He "alone" is master.

The returning king desires to be seen by his wife, making himself visible in the wake of the moment at which she wonders whether he has ever arrived. That the king wishes to be in power forever reflects his sense of having never been present. In the pivotal event of his childhood, on the verge of walking, he is not perceived by his father. His mother remains absent except for the instant at which she identifies him from a birthmark. At the end the king, in violent despair, seeks affirmation from the female eye and the face he has just struck.[23] The underlying story, then, articulates a yearning at the heart of terror.

4
Brüder Grimm
Der gläserne Sarg[24]

*S*age niemand daß ein armer Schneider es nicht weit bringen und nicht zu hohen Ehren gelangen könne, es ist weiter gar nichts nöthig als daß er an die rechte Schmiede kommt und, was die Hauptsache ist, daß es ihm glückt. Ein solches artiges und behendes Schneiderbürschchen gieng einmal seiner Wanderschaft nach und kam in einen großen Wald, und weil es den Weg nicht wußte, verirrte es sich. Die Nacht brach ein, und es blieb ihm nichts übrig als in dieser schauerlichen Einsamkeit ein Lager zu suchen. Auf dem weichen Mose hätte er freilich ein gutes Bett gefunden, allein die Furcht vor den wilden Thieren ließ ihm da keine Ruhe, und er mußte sich endlich entschließen auf einem Baume zu übernachten. Er suchte eine hohe Eiche, stieg bis in den Gipfel hinauf und dankte Gott daß er sein Bügeleisen bei sich trug, weil ihn sonst der Wind, der über die Gipfel der Bäume wehete, weggeführt hätte.

Nachdem er einige Stunden in der Finsternis, nicht ohne Zittern und Zagen, zugebracht hatte, erblickte er in geringer Entfernung den Schein eines Lichtes; und weil er dachte daß da eine menschliche Wohnung sein möchte, wo er sich besser befinden würde als auf den Ästen eines Baums, so stieg er vorsichtig herab und gieng dem Lichte nach. Es leitete ihn zu einem kleinen Häuschen, das aus Rohr und Binsen geflochten war. Er klopfte muthig an, die Thüre öffnete sich, und bei dem Scheine des herausfallenden Lichtes sah er ein altes eisgraues Männchen, das ein von buntfarbigen Lappen zusammengesetztes Kleid an hatte. 'Wer seid ihr, und was wollt ihr?' fragte es mit einer schnarrenden Stimme. 'Ich bin ein armer Schneider,' antwortete er, 'den die Nacht hier in der Wildnis überfallen hat, und bitte euch inständig mich bis Morgen in eurer Hütte aufzunehmen.' 'Geh deiner Wege,' erwiederte der Alte mit mürrischem Tone, 'mit Landstreichern will ich nichts zu schaffen haben; suche dir anderwärts ein Unterkommen.' Nach diesen

The Glass Coffin

No one ought to say that a poor tailor cannot go far and win high honors; nothing more at all is needed but that he get to the right place and, this being the most important matter, that things turn out luckily for him. Such a fine and nimble little tailor once went out on his wanderings, and came into a large forest, and because he did not know the way, he got lost. Night fell, and he had no choice but to look for a place to sleep in this dreadful solitude. He would of course have found a good bed on the soft moss, but his fear of the wild animals did not let him rest there, and finally he had to decide to spend the night in a tree. He looked for a tall oak, climbed to its top, and thanked God that he was carrying his flatiron with him, because otherwise the wind that blew over the treetops would have taken him away.

When he had spent a few hours in the darkness, not without trembling and trepidation, he saw the glimmer of a light shining nearby; and because he thought that a human dwelling might be there, where he would feel better than in the branches of a tree, he carefully descended and walked towards the light. It guided him to a little house woven of reeds and rushes. He knocked courageously, the door opened, and by the shine of the emanating light he saw an old, hoary little man who was wearing a garment composed of many-colored rags. "Who are you, and what do you want?" he asked in a raspy voice. "I am a poor tailor," he replied, "whom night has taken by surprise here in the wilderness, and I implore you to let me stay in your hut till tomorrow." "Go your way," the old man replied in a grumpy tone, "I do not want to have anything to do with vagabonds; look for shelter elsewhere." Following these words he wanted to slip into his house again, but the tailor held him by the corner of his garment and pleaded so movingly that the old

Worten wollte er wieder in sein Haus schlüpfen, aber der Schneider hielt ihn am Rockzipfel fest und bat so beweglich, daß der Alte, der so böse nicht war als er sich anstellte, endlich erweicht ward und ihn mit in seine Hütte nahm, wo er ihm zu essen gab und dann in einem Winkel ein ganz gutes Nachtlager anwies.

Der müde Schneider brauchte keines Einwiegens, sondern schlief sanft bis an den Morgen, würde auch noch nicht an das Aufstehen gedacht haben, wenn er nicht von einem lauten Lärm wäre aufgeschreckt worden. Ein heftiges Schreien und Brüllen drang durch die dünnen Wände des Hauses. Der Schneider, den ein unerwarteter Muth überkam, sprang auf, zog in der Hast seine Kleider an und eilte hinaus. Da erblickte er nahe bei dem Häuschen einen großen schwarzen Stier und einen schönen Hirsch, die in dem heftigsten Kampfe begriffen waren. Sie giengen mit so großer Wuth aufeinander los, daß von ihrem Getrampel der Boden erzitterte, und die Luft von ihrem Geschrei erdröhnte. Es war lange ungewis, welcher von beiden den Sieg davon tragen würde: endlich stieß der Hirsch seinem Gegner das Geweih in den Leib, worauf der Stier mit entsetzlichem Brüllen zur Erde sank, und durch einige Schläge des Hirsches völlig getödtet ward.

Der Schneider, welcher dem Kampfe mit Erstaunen zugesehen hatte, stand noch unbeweglich da, als der Hirsch in vollen Sprüngen auf ihn zu eilte und ihn, ehe er entfliehen konnte, mit seinem großen Geweihe geradezu aufgabelte. Er konnte sich nicht lange besinnen, denn es gieng schnellen Laufes fort über Stock und Stein, Berg und Thal, Wiese und Wald. Er hielt sich mit beiden Händen an die Enden des Geweihes fest und überließ sich seinem Schicksal. Es kam ihm aber nicht anders vor als flöge er davon. Endlich hielt der Hirsch vor einer Felsenwand still und ließ den Schneider sanft herabfallen. Der Schneider, mehr todt als lebendig, bedurfte längerer Zeit, um wieder zur Besinnung zu kommen. Als er sich einigermaßen erholt hatte, stieß der Hirsch, der neben ihm stehen geblieben war, sein Geweih mit solcher Gewalt gegen eine in dem Felsen befindliche Thüre, daß sie aufsprang. Feuerflammen schlugen heraus, auf welche ein großer Dampf folgte, der den Hirsch seinen Augen entzog. Der Schneider wußte nicht was er thun und wohin er sich wenden sollte, um aus dieser Einöde wieder unter Menschen zu gelangen. Indem er also unschlüssig stand, tönte eine Stimme aus dem Felsen, die ihm zurief 'tritt ohne Furcht herein, dir soll kein Leid widerfahren.' Er zauderte zwar, doch, von einer heimlichen Gewalt angetrieben,

man, who was not as mean as he made himself appear to be, softened at last and took him into his hut, where he gave him something to eat and then assigned him a rather good place to sleep in a corner.

The tired tailor did not need to be rocked, but slept peacefully till morning, and would not yet have thought of getting up if he had not been startled by a loud noise. A fierce screaming and roaring penetrated the thin walls of the house. The tailor, who was overcome by unexpected courage, leapt up, hastily put on his clothes, and rushed outside. There he saw a large black bull and a beautiful stag close to the little house, which were involved in the fiercest fight. They assailed each other with such great fury that the ground shook from their trampling and the air resounded with their screams. For a long time it was uncertain which of the two would gain the victory; finally the stag thrust his horns into his opponent's body, whereupon the bull fell to the ground with a dreadful roar and was finished off by a few blows from the stag.

The tailor, who had watched the fight with astonishment, was still standing there motionless when the stag came bounding toward him and, before he could escape, virtually picked him up with his large horns. He did not have much time to gather his thoughts, for the stag ran swiftly over hill and dale, mountain and valley, meadow and forest. He held on to the ends of the horns with both hands and abandoned himself to his fate. But it felt to him just as if he were flying away. Finally the stag stopped before a rock wall and let the tailor fall down gently. The tailor, more dead than alive, needed some time to come to his senses. When he had somewhat recuperated, the stag, which had remained standing by his side, thrust his horns with such force against a door in the rock that it sprang open. Flames of fire leapt out, followed by much smoke that removed the stag from his sight. The tailor did not know what to do or where to turn in order to get out of this wilderness and back to human beings. As he was thus standing there, not knowing what to do, a voice sounded from inside the rock, calling to him: "Enter without fear, you shall suffer no harm." He wavered, to be sure, but driven by a mysterious force, he obeyed the voice, and through an iron door reached a large, spacious hall whose ceiling, walls, and floor consisted of square stones polished to a shine, on each of which signs unknown to him were carved. He

gehorchte er der Stimme und gelangte durch die eiserne Thür in einen großen geräumigen Saal, dessen Decke, Wände und Boden aus glänzend geschliffenen Quadratsteinen bestanden, auf deren jedem ihm unbekannte Zeichen eingehauen waren. Er betrachtete alles voll Bewunderung und war eben in Begriff wieder hinaus zu gehen, als er abermals die Stimme vernahm, welche ihm sagte 'tritt auf den Stein, der in der Mitte des Saales liegt, und dein wartet großes Glück.'

Sein Muth war schon so weit gewachsen, daß er dem Befehle Folge leistete. Der Stein begann unter seinen Füßen nachzugeben und sank langsam in die Tiefe hinab. Als er wieder feststand, und der Schneider sich umsah, befand er sich in einem Saale, der an Umfang dem vorigen gleich war. Hier aber gab es mehr zu betrachten und zu bewundern. In die Wände waren Vertiefungen eingehauen, in welchen Gefäße von durchsichtigem Glase standen, die mit farbigem Spiritus oder mit einem bläulichen Rauche angefüllt waren. Auf dem Boden des Saales standen, einander gegenüber, zwei große gläserne Kasten, die sogleich seine Neugierde reizten. Indem er zu dem einen trat, erblickte er darin ein schönes Gebäude, einem Schlosse ähnlich, von Wirthschaftsgebäuden, Ställen und Scheuern und einer Menge anderer artigen Sachen umgeben. Alles war klein, aber überaus sorgfältig und zierlich gearbeitet, und schien von einer kunstreichen Hand mit der höchsten Genauigkeit ausgeschnitzt zu sein.

Er würde seine Augen von der Betrachtung dieser Seltenheiten noch nicht abgewendet haben, wenn sich nicht die Stimme abermals hätte hören lassen. Sie forderte ihn auf sich umzukehren und den gegenüberstehenden Glaskasten zu beschauen. Wie stieg seine Verwunderung als er darin ein Mädchen von größter Schönheit erblickte. Es lag wie im Schlafe, und war in lange blonde Haare wie in einen kostbaren Mantel eingehüllt. Die Augen waren fest geschlossen, doch die lebhafte Gesichtsfarbe und ein Band, das der Athem hin und her bewegte, ließen keinen Zweifel an ihrem Leben. Der Schneider betrachtete die Schöne mit klopfendem Herzen, als sie plötzlich die Augen aufschlug und bei seinem Anblick in freudigem Schrecken zusammenfuhr. 'Gerechter Himmel,' rief sie, 'meine Befreiung naht! geschwind, geschwind, hilf mir aus meinem Gefängnis: wenn du den Riegel an diesem gläsernen Sarg wegschiebst, so bin ich erlöst.' Der Schneider gehorchte ohne Zaudern, alsbald hob sie den Glasdeckel in die Höhe, stieg heraus und eilte in die Ecke des Saals, wo sie sich in einen weiten Mantel verhüllte. Dann setzte

regarded everything full of admiration, and was on the verge of leaving when once again he heard the voice, which told him: "Step upon the stone that lies in the middle of the hall: great good fortune awaits you."

His courage had already grown so much that he followed the command. The stone began to give way under his feet, and slowly sank down into the depths. When it stood still again and the tailor looked around, he was in a hall whose size equaled that of the previous one. Here, however, there was more to be regarded and admired. In the walls recesses had been carved, in which stood vessels of transparent glass filled with colored spirit or with a bluish smoke. On the floor of the hall there stood, opposite each other, two large glass cases, which at once aroused his curiosity. As he went to one of them, he saw therein a beautiful edifice similar to a castle, and surrounded by farm buildings, stables, and barns, and a lot of other fine things. Everything was small, but made most carefully and delicately—carved, it seemed, with the greatest precision by an artful hand.

He would not yet have taken his eyes off these rarities, if the voice had not resounded once more. It asked him to turn around and to regard the glass case that stood on the opposite side. How his astonishment grew when he saw therein a most beautiful maiden! She lay as if asleep, and was enveloped in long, blond hair as if in a precious cloak. Her eyes were firmly shut, but her lively complexion and a ribbon, which her breathing moved back and forth, left no doubt that she was alive. With pounding heart, the tailor was gazing at the beauty when suddenly she opened her eyes and at the sight of him started with joyful fright. "Good heavens," she exclaimed, "my liberation is near! Quick, quick, help me out of my prison: if you push back the bolt on this glass coffin, I will be saved." The tailor obeyed without hesitation, and thereupon she lifted the glass lid, stepped out, and rushed to a corner of the hall, where she covered herself with a large cloak. Then she sat down on a stone, and told the young man to step up to her; and after she had given him a friendly kiss on his lips, she said: "My long-desired savior, good Heaven has led you to me and put an end to my sufferings. On the same day on which they end, your good fortune shall begin. You are my husband, destined for me by heaven, and you shall spend your life in unfettered joy, loved by me and showered with every earthly possession. Sit down and listen to the story of my fate.

sie sich auf einen Stein nieder, hieß den jungen Mann heran gehen, und nachdem sie einen freundlichen Kuß auf seinen Mund gedrückt hatte, sprach sie 'mein lang ersehnter Befreier, der gütige Himmel hat mich zu dir geführt und meinen Leiden ein Ziel gesetzt. An demselben Tage, wo sie endigen, soll dein Glück beginnen. Du bist der vom Himmel bestimmte Gemahl, und sollst, von mir geliebt und mit allen irdischen Gütern überhäuft, in ungestörter Freud dein Leben zubringen. Sitz nieder und höre die Erzählung meines Schicksals.

'Ich bin die Tochter eines reichen Grafen. Meine Eltern starben als ich noch in zarter Jugend war und empfahlen mich in ihren letzten Willen meinem ältern Bruder, bei dem ich auferzogen wurde. Wir liebten uns so zärtlich und waren so übereinstimmend in unserer Denkungsart und unsern Neigungen, daß wir beide den Entschluß faßten uns niemals zu verheirathen, sondern bis an das Ende unseres Lebens beisammen zu bleiben. In unserm Hause war an Gesellschaft nie Mangel: Nachbarn und Freunde besuchten uns häufig, und wir übten gegen alle die Gastfreundschaft in vollem Maße. So geschah es auch eines Abends, daß ein Fremder in unser Schloß geritten kam und, unter dem Vorgeben den nächsten Ort nicht mehr erreichen zu können, um ein Nachtlager bat. Wir gewährten seine Bitte mit zuvorkommender Höflichkeit, und er unterhielt uns während des Abendessens mit seinem Gespräche und eingemischten Erzählungen auf das anmuthigste. Mein Bruder hatte ein so großes Wohlgefallen an ihm, daß er ihn bat ein paar Tage bei uns zu verweilen, wozu er nach einigem Weigern einwilligte. Wir standen erst spät in der Nacht vom Tische auf, dem Fremden wurde ein Zimmer angewiesen, und ich eilte, ermüdet wie ich war, meine Glieder in die weichen Federn zu senken. Kaum war ich ein wenig eingeschlummert, so weckten mich die Töne einer zarten und lieblichen Musik. Da ich nicht begreifen konnte woher sie kamen, so wollte ich mein im Nebenzimmer schlafendes Kammermädchen rufen, allein zu meinem Erstaunen fand ich daß mir, als lastete ein Alp auf meiner Brust, von einer unbekannten Gewalt die Sprache benommen und ich unvermögend war den geringsten Laut von mir zu geben. Indem sah ich bei dem Schein der Nachtlampe den Fremden in mein durch zwei Thüren fest verschlossenes Zimmer eintreten. Er näherte sich mir und sagte daß er durch Zauberkräfte, die ihm zu Gebote ständen, die liebliche Musik habe ertönen lassen um mich aufzuwecken, und dringe jetzt selbst durch alle Schlösser in der Absicht, mir Herz und Hand anzubieten. Mein

"I am the daughter of a rich count. My parents died when I was still in my tender youth, and recommended me in their Last Wills to my older brother, by whom I was raised. We loved each other so tenderly and agreed so much in our way of thinking and our inclinations that both of us decided never to marry, but to stay together to the end of our lives. In our house, there never was a lack of company: neighbors and friends visited us often, and we extended our hospitality to everyone in full measure. And so it happened one evening that a stranger came riding into our castle and, under the pretense of not being able to still reach the next town, asked for a place to sleep. We granted his request with great politeness, and at dinner he entertained us most gracefully with his conversation and intermingled tales. My brother took such a delight in him that he asked him to stay with us for a few days, which he accepted after some reluctance. We rose from the table only late at night, the stranger was shown to a room, and tired as I was, I rushed to rest my limbs on my soft feather bed. Hardly had I fallen into a bit of slumber when I was awoken by the sound of tender and lovely music. As I was not able to determine from where it was coming, I wanted to call my chambermaid who slept in the adjoining room, but to my astonishment I found that an unknown force had taken speech away from me, as if a nightmare were weighing on my chest, and that I was unable to utter the slightest sound. Meanwhile, by the light of the night lamp, I saw the stranger enter into my room whose two doors were tightly locked. He approached me and said that by magic powers that were at his disposal he had prompted the lovely music to sound in order to wake me up, and that now he himself was penetrating through all the locks with the intention of offering me his heart and hand. My revulsion at his magic arts, however, was so great that I did not answer him at all. For a time, he stood there without moving, probably with the intention of waiting for an advantageous decision, but when I continued to be silent, he furiously declared that he would revenge himself and find some means to punish my haughtiness, whereupon he left the room. I spent the night in the greatest restlessness and only toward morning fell into a slumber. When I had awoken, I rushed to my brother to tell him what had happened, but I did not find him in his room, and his attendant told me that he had ridden out to hunt with the stranger at daybreak.

Widerwille aber gegen seine Zauberkünste war so groß, daß ich ihn keiner Antwort würdigte. Er blieb eine Zeit lang unbeweglich stehen, wahrscheinlich in der Absicht einen günstigen Entschluß zu erwarten, als ich aber fortfuhr zu schweigen, erklärte er zornig daß er sich rächen und Mittel finden werde meinen Hochmuth zu bestrafen, worauf er das Zimmer wieder verließ. Ich brachte die Nacht in höchster Unruhe zu und schlummerte erst gegen Morgen ein. Als ich erwacht war, eilte ich zu meinem Bruder, um ihn von dem was vorgefallen war zu benachrichtigen, allein ich fand ihn nicht auf seinem Zimmer, und der Bediente sagte mir daß er bei anbrechendem Tage mit dem Fremden auf die Jagd geritten sei.

Mir ahnete gleich nichts gutes. Ich kleidete mich schnell an, ließ meinen Leibzelter satteln und ritt, nur von einem Diener begleitet, in vollem Jagen nach dem Walde. Der Diener stürzte mit dem Pferde und konnte mir, da das Pferd den Fuß gebrochen hatte, nicht folgen. Ich setzte, ohne mich aufzuhalten, meinen Weg fort, und in wenigen Minuten sah ich den Fremden mit einem schönen Hirsch, den er an der Linie führte, auf mich zukommen. Ich fragte ihn wo er meinen Bruder gelassen habe und wie er zu diesem Hirsche gelangt sei, aus dessen großen Augen ich Thränen fließen sah. Anstatt mir zu antworten fieng er an laut aufzulachen. Ich gerieth darüber in höchsten Zorn, zog eine Pistole und drückte sie gegen das Ungeheuer ab, aber die Kugel prallte von seiner Brust zurück und fuhr in den Kopf meines Pferdes. Ich stürzte zur Erde, und der Fremde murmelte einige Worte, die mir das Bewußtsein raubten.

Als ich wieder zur Besinnung kam fand ich mich in dieser unterirdischen Gruft in einem gläsernen Sarge. Der Schwarzkünstler erschien nochmals, sagte daß er meinen Bruder in einen Hirsch verwandelt, mein Schloß, mit allem Zubehör, verkleinert, in den andern Glaskasten eingeschlossen, und meine in Rauch verwandelten Leute in Glasflaschen gebannt hätte. Wolle ich mich jetzt seinem Wunsche fügen, so sei ihm ein leichtes, alles wieder in den vorigen Stand zu setzen: er brauche nur die Gefäße zu öffnen, so werde alles wieder in die natürliche Gestalt zurückkehren. Ich antwortete ihm so wenig als das erste Mal. Er verschwand und ließ mich in meinem Gefängnisse liegen, in welchem mich ein tiefer Schlaf befiel. Unter den Bildern, welche an meiner Seele vorübergiengen, war auch das tröstliche, daß ein junger Mann kam und mich befreite, und als ich heute die Augen öffne, so erblicke ich dich und sehe meinen Traum erfüllt. Hilf mir vollbringen was in jenem Gesichte

At once I did not sense anything good. I dressed quickly, had my horse saddled and rode, accompanied only by a servant, at full speed toward the forest. The servant fell with his horse, and was not able to follow me, because his horse had broken its foot. Without further ado, I continued on my way, and in a few minutes I saw the stranger coming toward me with a beautiful stag, which he led by a leash. I asked him where he had left my brother and how he had acquired this stag, from whose big eyes I saw tears flow. Instead of answering me, he started to laugh loudly. At that I flew into a most intense rage, drew a pistol, and fired at the monster, but the bullet bounced back from his chest and went into the head of my horse. I fell to the ground, and the stranger murmured several words, which robbed me of my consciousness.

When I came to my senses, I found myself in a glass coffin in this underground tomb. The sorcerer appeared once again, and said that he had transformed my brother into a stag, had locked up a shrunk version of my castle with all of its parts in the other glass case, and had imprisoned my people — transformed into smoke — in glass vessels. If I now were to give in to his desire, it would be easy for him to put everything back into its previous state: he would only need to open the vessels, and everything would return to its natural shape. I answered him as little as I had the first time. He vanished and left me lying in my prison, in which I fell into a deep sleep. Among the images that passed by my soul, there was the consoling one in which a young man came and liberated me, and when I opened my eyes today, I saw you and saw my dream fulfilled. Help me achieve what further happened in that vision. First, let us lift the glass case in which my castle is contained onto that wide stone."

As soon as the weight had been put on the stone, it began to rise and, with the maiden and the young man, ascended through the opening of the ceiling into the upper hall, where they then were easily able to reach the open air. There the maiden opened the lid, and it was wonderful to regard how the castle, the houses, and the farmsteads expanded and grew back to their natural size with the greatest rapidity. Then they went back to the underground cave and had the smoke-filled glasses carried up by the stone. No sooner had the maiden opened the bottles when the blue smoke rushed out and transformed into living human beings, in whom the maiden recognized her servants and people. Her joy increased even more when her brother, who

noch weiter geschah. Das erste ist daß wir den Glaskasten, in welchem mein Schloß sich befindet, auf jenen breiten Stein heben.'

Der Stein, sobald er beschwert war, hob sich mit dem Fräulein und dem Jüngling in die Höhe, und stieg durch die Öffnung der Decke in den obern Saal, wo sie dann leicht ins Freie gelangen konnten. Hier öffnete das Fräulein den Deckel, und es war wunderbar anzusehen, wie Schloß, Häuser und Gehöfte sich ausdehnten und in größter Schnelligkeit zu natürlicher Größe heranwuchsen. Sie kehrten darauf in die unterirdische Höhle zurück und ließen die mit Rauch gefüllten Gläser von dem Steine herauftragen. Kaum hatte das Fräulein die Flaschen geöffnet, so drang der blaue Rauch heraus und verwandelte sich in lebendige Menschen, in welchen das Fräulein ihre Diener und Leute erkannte. Ihre Freude ward noch vermehrt als ihr Bruder, der den Zauberer in dem Stier getödtet hatte, in menschlicher Gestalt aus dem Walde heran kam, und noch denselben Tag reichte das Fräulein, ihrem Versprechen gemäß, dem glücklichen Schneider die Hand am Altare.

had killed the magician in the form of the bull, came out of the forest in human shape; and on the very same day the maiden, following her promise, gave the happy tailor her hand at the altar.

5

Skins of a Tale: "The Glass Coffin"

> The spoken word, and even more, the written word, has the power to function as a skin.
>
> DIDIER ANZIEU
> *Le Moi-peau*

In "The Glass Coffin," luck and catastrophe dwell in each other's utter proximity.[25] As the plot progresses toward its happy ending, a story beside the tale evolves at limits of insight and linguistic articulation. As do all such stories, it resists the pressures of thesis-driven interpretations. Reading and understanding "The Glass Coffin" involves sensibilities before and beyond conceptual closure. At edges of silence, the organ of touch and a sensorily inflected consciousness come alive. An affective awareness emanates from envelopmental inscriptions and dermatic exposure. Terror and delight interweave strangely here, with an insistence that both attracts and defies comprehension. The very small steps of the very close readings to follow negotiate uncertain grounds.

The tale's plot has a tailor discover, to his surprise and delight, a beautiful young woman locked in a glass case. She implores him to free her, he unlocks the case without hesitation, and she announces that he is "destined" (37) to become her husband. Events progress with breathtaking speed, and at the same time, it appears, all clocks have stopped. In that realm of timelessness, the realities and the fictions attain a new freshness and fluidity. Emotions come to the fore. They transport the tale into a space where boundaries are crossed and lives recast. On the way to this extraordinary—and precarious—situation, the young man hears a voice from a wall of rock asking him to turn around and look at the glass behind him. He is gripped by astonishment at what he sees. The "most beautiful maiden" lies there "as if asleep" (37).

Terror in the Tale: Narrative Compression and Unpredictability

The female protagonist seems to be at rest when she is actually conscious. But is she truly awake in spite of her semblance? As we regard her, we see clear signs of genuine slumber. Her eyes are firmly closed, and there is no movement other than that of a ribbon shifting back and forth in the rhythm of her breath. Lying there, then, she may be asleep or not. Uncertainty pervades the zone at the wall and the case. We also do not know what exactly the young man has heard from the wall—is it a voice or an echo?

Once distinctly awake, the female figure calls the case a "glass coffin" (37). The case, in which she lies as if on exhibition under the sway of death, appears to be an instrument of incarceration. "The Glass Coffin" remains curiously opaque with regard to her experience. The "heavens" have sent her "savior." Nevertheless, an anxiety, even a terror makes itself felt. Upon opening her eyes, the woman in the case is seized by "joyful terror," as Margaret Hunt perceived in her translation (241). Terror is noted, but it is coupled with joy—and momently disappears.

Yet a deeply felt, if scattered, sense of peril emanates from the narrative. When ambiguities arise, the narrator quickly asserts that the ribbon's motion on the woman's chest as well as her fresh complexion "left no doubt that she was alive" (37). However, no such question was raised before. For another moment, the specter of death enters into the obscurity around sleep and wakefulness. Looking into the glass container, the young man sees more than an individual appearance. He is drawn into a fluid realm where the body acquires the radiance of the instant in which it lives, and passes on forever.

As the tale begins with the wanderings of the young man, night falls in the forest. The dread of being torn apart by wild beasts drives the "little tailor" (33) to the top of an oak tree. Up there, however, another hazard awaits him, a powerful wind that threatens to blow him off. But a tool of his trade, an iron that adds to his weight, prevents the tailor from being "taken...away." Without that tool, the tale might come to an early halt, or else take a turn "away." In such potential circumstances, the tailor may vanish, or take us far away beyond the horizon. With these possibilities of his premature departure, the "it," "es" (32), as which he was initially introduced—a small, somewhat genderless figure—reappears. Past the tale, in far-off skies, this figure belongs to a wind beyond narrative control: "it" behaves unpredictably—it may never again materialize, or return to grip us in the next sentence.

Far-fetched as such eventualities may seem, they resonate with another tale in the Grimms' collection, "The Giant and the Tailor." There the protagonist, another tailor, is outwitted by a "sky-high tower" (KHM II, 361)[26] later recognized as a giant, who asks him to sit down on a willow branch so that he may prove weighty enough to bend it. Having rushed onto such a branch, the little man holds his breath. With the air inside his lungs, he succeeds in the venture. Yet when he has to catch another breath, he is catapulted high into the sky, beyond anyone's vision.

That tale ends with a variation on the happy ending ascribed to fairy-tale romance: "If he has not fallen down again, he must still be floating about in the air." His "bad luck"—"Unglück" (KHM II, 363)—the tale reasons, stems from not having put his iron into his pocket. The narrative's rationale, however, falls short of its suggestive reach. Floating high in the air, the tailor is both invisible and persistently present. As long as the narrative ends as it does, it may begin once again upon a time.

The course of events in these tales, then, hardly illuminates their range of imagination. In "The Glass Coffin," the fear of the beasts and the power of the storm enter into an underlying emotional fabric from the very beginning. In the opening sentence, the tailor's levity and the circumstance that keeps his body on the spot are preconstellated: "No one ought to say that a poor tailor cannot go far and win high honors; nothing more at all is needed but that he get to the right place" —literally: "forge," "Schmiede"—"and, this being the most important matter, that things turn out luckily for him" ("Sage niemand daß ein armer Schneider es nicht weit bringen und nicht zu hohen Ehren gelangen könne, es ist weiter gar nichts nöthig als daß er an die rechte

Schmiede kommt und, was die Hauptsache ist, daß es ihm glückt" [32]).

Although the idiomatic forge comes forth only at the narrative's onset, a dynamic of compression surfaces time and again. Having originated in a forge, the iron that keeps the tailor and the tale on course stands in the service of pressing. Its weight counteracts his lightness. In his levity and at the surfaces that delineate his physique, the tailor is vulnerable to the pressures of his environment. Unless it is established delicately, contact with the outside world puts him at risk. Before he is seized by fear and exposed to the wind, the "soft moss" of the forest offers itself as "a good bed" (33). But the forge of the tale awaits him instead, along with a particular kind of luck. The right "forge" is needed in order to be successful, but above all good luck is required, the initial sentence seems to announce.

A peculiar "es" (32), "it," however, subverts the order of the dominant tale. "Es" performs its work so subtly that the laboring translator is bound to catch it in return for stylistic oddity or—as has been done customarily—to drop it altogether. "All that is needed," Hunt translates, "is that we should go to the right smithy, and what is of most consequence, that we should have good luck" (238). With Manheim: "All he has to do is get to the right place at the right time and, most important of all, have good luck" (507). However, nothing less than the workings of luck are qualified by "it," "the most important matter" being that "things"—"it"—"turn out luckily for him" (33). Having good luck is not a requirement per se for faring well. Luck cannot be had. Whatever "it" is that needs to turn out well with the help of good fortune—we receive no specific wording on it. Already in this early experience, "it" evokes forces beyond narrative command. The tailor's fear of the wind a few sentences further emanates from this inception at the edge of speechlessness.

The possibility of "it" turning out luckily forms the threshold of a story beyond bounds, but also of obscurely shaped delimitations. "It" could be anything; the tale about it will perform its movements less than a step away from something that eludes its grasp. "Luck," "Glück," which as a noun and subject exudes a certain objectivity, does not even occur around the "it." Instead we find the verbal inflection, "glückt," suggesting potential happenings for "it," "es." In their range between hope and doom, "es" and "glückt" form an elusive pair. The sky of flight extends endlessly for "it," the little tailor, as well as "it," the subject of lucky verbalization. But this very flight may turn into unspeakable loss in an instant. In such a case, the tailor and "the most important matter" would vanish without account.

All the more the tale seeks to create a ground on which to proceed. Having succeeded in staying close to the earth, thanks to the iron, the tailor gives thanks to God. He addresses an ultimate authority. In the wake of this thanksgiving, the heavens of boundless flight are subjected to the workings of the universal forge. The powerful name reduces "it" in its intractable indeterminacy.

The dominant tale seems to gain strength from the self-assuredness of proverbial knowledge as well. "Everybody is their own fortune's smith," "jeder ist seines Glückes Schmied," brings up the image of some right smithy the tailor should reach in due time. Could he author his own luck, a grateful particle in an authorial universe? The tailor's potential luck, however, differs dramatically from a fortune of one's own. Although the "right forge," "rechte Schmiede" (32), and his life might be blessed with luck—if "it" works out well—the tailor is not in charge of his own future. What matters is that it turns out luckily "for" (33), not through him. Less determined than "everybody" in the proverb, "it" is the decisive context in which luck needs to favor "him." To the extent that "it" cannot be cast in a specific form or meaning, it counteracts the tale's compressive thrust. "It" will be determined by lucky circumstance and cannot be invoked as a particular goal. The dominant tale sets out on its course as announced. "It," however, remains to be seen in its unpredictable configurations: a story beside the tale signals its presence.

Tales Breathe through Their Pores

A lucky circumstance provides the tailor with safe lodging for the night: he sees a light. Although the tailor has spent several hours in its immediate vicinity, he notices it only now. Something important and close to him had escaped his attention. Later, when he suddenly becomes aware of the glass case, physical proximity again turns out to be of pivotal significance. In each instance, the narrative takes a decisive turn once this protagonist has taken note of his surroundings. He wakes up to what has been there all along. His consciousness is aroused at those moments. After seeing the light, he "thought" —"dachte" (32)—of a "human dwelling" (33), and the sight of the case jolts him out of a meditative mood. In each occurrence, a specific narrative situation opens up unexpectedly. The tailor had been stuck in the tree, but then searches for a new source of support; his attention had been captured by a miniature replica of a country estate, but then he sets out toward the young woman.

Lucky circumstance vis-à-vis a strongly defined situation is at work in each case. A sense of compression and, in the latter event, of contraction precedes the liberating developments. Small sizes and spaces come into play along with good fortune. The "most important matter" (33) of the lucky turn springs from seemingly minor dimensions. Yet the dominant narrative forges ahead as if explicit orientation and the big events of the plot were decisive. As an adventure tale with its lessons for young and old, "The Glass Coffin" presents a forge of life. Yet once we awake to the sights and sounds underneath and around the dominant tale, different wonders and fears appear: a story in its small and nevertheless strongly consequential dimensions relates life, and contingencies of death, under the sway of fortune.

Following the light, the tailor finds a little old man wearing a coat of many-colored patches. Like his visitor before him, this figure is introduced as an "it," "es" (32). "It" speaks with a voice called "raspy" ("schnarrenden" [32]), and thus expresses itself in a manner that is more evocative and less defined than speech in its clear-cut variations. When the door to the old man's hut first opens, defined perceptions and identities fade as well. The light from inside the hut falls out at the man, and its "shine" ("Scheine" [32]) reveals "it," an "old, hoary" (33) being. This light is not merely illuminating the scene, but setting it somewhere between appearance and a more factual presence. *Schein* denotes the shine of a light, and a semblance.

In this uncertain atmosphere, the old man poses an ultimate question: "Who are you, and what do you want?" (33). On the level of the plot, the response is honest enough: "I am a poor tailor...whom night has taken by surprise here in the wilderness, and I implore you to let me stay in your hut till tomorrow." Fittingly, the man sends him back onto the path of events: "Go your way…" Yet the tailor holds on; he clings to a corner of the many-colored coat. In doing so, he activates his smaller self. "It" attaches itself to the garment like an infant to a mother. "It" is in touch with something very small and very significant. Larger entities, abstractions like "night" (33) and "wilderness," "Wildnis" (32), fade into the background.

What matters at this moment is the corner of a coat whose patches derive from many and uncertain places. Uncertainty—its risks and possibilities—pervades the narrative throughout. Good fortune is near when the tailor engages concretely and attentively with his immediate environment. He saw the light nearby. Now he is close to home. The tailor pins his hopes onto the edge of a coat. His manner of speaking changes. Rather than presenting himself as a subject wishing to move from the night and wilderness into the hut, he now pleads "movingly" (33), speaks from the heart. The hardened reality of the forge wanes: "At last" the old man "softened" (35). He offers a corner of his hut, and a meal for which the tailor had not asked.

Life at the margins is highly unpredictable. The hut is woven of "reeds and rushes" (33), its walls are thin. Through them, luck may strike, and so may calamity. The tailor has moved further into a narrative of suspended goals and surprising arrivals. Well-rested and fed, he is ready for nothing in particular. When his sleep ends because of a violent commotion outside the hut, he is "overcome by unexpected courage" (35). Valor takes hold of him like unforeseeable fortune. A changed protagonist emerges from the hut. The time of the iron has passed. The tailor does not hold on to where he is. Before he has a chance to think about what is happening, he feels "as if he were flying away." He does not resist this experience, as he did in the fear of the wind. Instead, captured by a stag, he abandons himself to his "fate." At the "ends of the horns" (35), rather than stuck on a tree, the tailor is in fast motion, wherever it might take him. The courage that seized him is amplified to a limit. At this limit, "it" is near, someone whose specific identity does not matter, someone—something—beyond "his" scope.

Transformed beyond his will, moving with the winds of fortune, this figure develops certain sensibilities and shapes. The workings of the forge impart a two-dimensional quality to the tailor, a slender figure to begin with. With his depth reduced, his periphery gains in significance. It is there that the wind may capture him, as if he were a sail. He in turn latches onto peripheries—the edge of a garment, the ends of antlers. At such boundaries, a hidden story can be felt. Horns threaten to pierce the tailor's clothing and skin and, in a seemingly more positive vein, the woman in and out of the coffin engages him through several enclosures—the glass, her long hair wrapped all around her, her "lively complexion" (37), and most intimately through her exposed body, her naked skin, which she rushes to cover as soon as she has stepped out of the case.

The tale falls silent before this exposure. The woman's "entirely naked" state resonates in her haste, but is not admitted into direct expression. In his published version, which closely follows the Baroque novel[27] from which he adapted the tale, Wilhelm Grimm struck this characterization as well as her depiction as "the beautiful naked one." But in physical and metaphorical skins, a story is inscribed. Looking at these skins, we see peripheral textures at limits of language. As we write of these textures, the power of linguistic signification fades. Skin language eludes referential networks. The tailor's astonishment before the coffin speaks, but not his tongue. He sees the body inside, and never again in this tale utters a word. In the wake of the woman's appearance, a silence increasingly articulates itself, his as well as hers. It is the silence of the story that nevertheless communicates.

The smallest patch of textual skin comes alive when touched. If neglected in its miniscule, unrulily mobile manifestations, the story beside the tale goes unnoticed. The small spaces of storytelling matter. Tales breathe through their pores. Once, then, there was a tailor in the wind, pressed like a garment, fastened to an oak like a sail, "not without trembling and trepidation," "nicht ohne Zittern und Zagen" (32). Fear and trepidation register on an oscillating surface. No longer is he advancing on his way through the world. Held in place at the treetop, but precariously so, his connection with the ground may rupture in the course of the night.

The narrative opens up toward a reader's, listener's, infant's vertiginous nightmare. The skin of the earth tears open and releases them who fly off toward nowhere in particular. The "solitude" in which this episode occurs evokes a shudder, "Schauer," of its own; it is "schauerlich" (32). "Soft moss," however, offers "a good bed" (33), somewhat porous, like skin, and responsive to bodily contours. Yet the dread of the beasts prevails. He might be shredded, skin and all. Feeling dramatically vulnerable, but nevertheless resilient in crisis, the tailor moves into a second skin, the hut of "reeds and rushes" (33), with its walls as thin as a coat. In the morning a violent noise "penetrated," "drang durch" (34), the texture. Before the garment maker knows what is happening to him, he is "virtually picked...up" ("geradezu aufgabelte" [34], literally: "forked up") and once again at risk of being shredded. The beast beyond his control assails his professional surface, so to speak: in the fork's figurative dimension, the textile skin manufactured by his trade is pierced. Circumstance, luck's fickle cousin, takes its turn.

Narrative Membranes

In the rapid movement on top of the horns, the narrative breaks away from the tense dichotomy between heaven and earth. The tailor is not caught any more between the possibility of boundless passage into space and the downward pressures of the forge, as he was on top of the tree. Riding on the horns, he is in the uncontrollable sphere of fortune. In the air above the racing, agitated animal, it appears to him "as if he were flying away" (35). His experience continues to resonate in the realm of the skin.[28] If the image of a sail composed of clothes and skin arose at the treetop, it readily returns on the horns—it is as if he were sailing through the air. But this time he does not resist the force of nature. The stag, which has just pierced the bull's skin, pushed his antlers into its body, and struck dead the collapsed, screaming animal, belongs among the beasts from which the tailor sought refuge on the treetop; now he finds himself on the beast, an "it" again rather than a rider in charge. He "abandoned himself to his fate" (35), the text reads. As before, this evocation of fate and—as it turns out—good luck is preceded by a sense of compression. "Virtually forked up," the tailor is subjected to intense pressure before taking off. The forge of life exercises its power, but on the verge of being pierced, he in the next moment is in luck. Or so it seems: flying away in itself will not necessarily bring good fortune to the tailor. There is no indication at all where the stag might take him. The animal drops him in front of a rock wall, but even then he hardly knows where he is. "More dead than alive" (35), he regains full consciousness only after a while.

Before the plot moves forward to a different location, the extralinear narrative unfolds on the spot. Sensibilities of the skin continue to register as the tailor falls "gently" (35) onto the ground before the wall, where he rests as he might have on the moss at the beginning. No longer is he afraid of the beasts. A wild and powerful animal, the stag, stands next to the tailor as he recuperates from the flight of fortune. Lying on a "good bed" (33), if the gentle descent includes his arrival on the ground, the tailor experiences a promising, precarious uncertainty. Suspended between consciousness and an immobility akin to death, he is gathering strength for the story that awaits him. In this state, he senses little more than the contours of his body alongside the ground.

Once the tailor has returned to a more encompassing consciousness—away from an awareness along points of enclosure and physical contact—a voice from the rock asks him to walk through a door in the wall. He "wavered" (35), and in this vacillation the "trembling and trepidation" from the earlier treetop is recalled. "Fear" (33, 35) expressly occurs in both situations, but the tailor in front of the door is experienced in the jolts of fortune, and has passed through the woven abode. Emotionally evolved, the story now affects both sides of the skin: in his wavering, the tailor will be trembling within and without. The wavering responds to an obscure voice that then drives the protagonist through the door in conjunction with "a mysterious force" (35). On the other side there is a large spacious hall "whose ceiling, walls, and floor consisted of square stones polished to a shine, on each of which signs unknown to him were carved" (35). An unknown language presents itself, and in its obscurity it speaks.

This unknown, then, contains elements of the enshrouded story. The tale manifests clearly enough in the plot; the story communicates through an insistently affective, at times enigmatic idiom. The voice that induces the tailor to step into the hall springs from the "great good fortune" that "awaits" (37) the protagonist somewhere past the tale. References to the unknown and to mysterious signs create an expectation that the tale, tied to a string of happenings as it is, will not be able to fulfill. In this expectation, the edges of the tale and the story's outer layers coincide. A narrative membrane delimits the tale on one side, and on its other the story.

Exiting from the hall, the tailor stands on a rock that slowly sinks downward. In this movement the risks of being pierced violently or pressed upon with force fade away; "good fortune," "luck," is promised instead. The obscurely enduring story asserts itself in stages. The hall forms an evocative space and container. In his perceptions, the tailor is transported back and forth through the membrane between this space and elements of the story in the tale before. The hall encloses sights as a skin would, and like this organ it does not do so hermetically.

Wherever the tailor looks in the hall, he sees stones into which signs unknown to him have been "carved" (35) with the considerable force required to imprint such forms on hard matter. The forge of the proverb comes to mind, but the heart of this matter is mysterious like the workings of luck. From the compressed space created in the carving of the letters, encrypted communications issue forth, and once again the dynamics of the forge bring about possibilities beyond pressure. The story blossoms in this reversal. The tailor gazes at the signs with deep "admiration," "Bewunderung" (36), an activity prefiguring his "astonishment," "Verwunderung" (36), at the sight of the coffin. The story continues to speak in linguistic modulations. Sounds and rhythms link kindred words, feelings, and perceptions. With the story, a language in flux unfolds.

Square stones are no impediment for the workings of the story. Tales build fairy-tale castles of such sturdy material, with tightly locked forbidden rooms on rocky, remote mountaintops. The story does otherwise. Its stones are polished to a shine. Exquisitely smooth planes delimit the three dimensions of the hall; in its shine, each stone generates a sense of surface. Such planes of enclosure speak more intensely than their three-dimensional building blocks. The image of the sail, of its flatness, reappears. At the same time the story asserts its evolution. Before the stones the tailor is gripped by wonderment. The signs embody endless possibilities. Limitless horizons, however, are not among the potential sights any more. The specter of the tailor in the air, a sail in the wind, does not arise here. Shiny surfaces envelop him, like skin.

Affective Awareness

As the image of the sail returns and transforms at the hall's peripheries, so does the shine that stilled the tailor's fear of the wind above the trees, and of the beasts on the ground. "Polished to a shine" (35), the enigmatically inscribed stones exude both firmness, the strength of the hall, and—in the wide array of meanings attached to them—potentiality. In their presence and suggestiveness, these stones revive the "shine" (33), *Schein*, emanating from the earlier woven hut, and then falling across its threshold as the door opens. The story has developed meanwhile. At the door, someone appeared whose emotional presence the tailor, clutching the garment before him, needed to acknowledge before receiving shelter and nourishment. In the hall, he is more affectively involved to begin with: he "regarded," "betrachtete" (36), the unknown signs "full of admiration" (37).

His courage undergoes a similar development and transformation. He had knocked at the door of the hut "courageously," "muthig" (32). Later, hearing the violent noise at the end of the night, he had been "overcome" (35) by a courage, "Muth" (34), no longer his own. Finally, in the hall, his courage has "grown" (37) to the point where he is strongly receptive to the mysterious voice. Courage has taken hold in him like a plant, and simultaneously it is activated through an outside agency whose nature he does not know. An inner emotional and an outer, acoustically defined energy coalesce, at an affective and perceptual boundary akin to skin. The rock stepped upon in this spirit turns into a threshold toward another cavern, underneath the hall of the signs. With the tailor on top, it "slowly sank down into the depths" (37). The rock moves down into another space rather than exerting a forge-like pressure. It is an instrument of "great good fortune" (37), as the voice had predicted. It does not form a threshold across which the tailor would step as he did from the outside into the hut. Rather the rock moves downward along the demarcation line formed by and between the voice and the tailor's emotional presence. The story's boundary, its skin, remains intact and evolves in this movement.

Movements into a significant depth characterize the tale and the story throughout. The tailor finds the woman in the coffin underneath the earth, in the cavern below the underground hall. His downward course begins on the treetop from which he descends to the hut and his resting place on the ground. Depth in "The Glass Coffin," however, is not limited to geocentric dimensions. The treetop forms a potential point of departure into outer space. Rather than moving toward the ground and into the earth, the tailor may fly off, never to be seen again. If the depths of the universe and those of the planet coalesce in this configuration, the tailor again appears precariously lodged on a line of demarcation. Literally and figuratively, he has little ground to stand on. The space he may traverse from this location stretches the limits of imagination. On the treetop—and elsewhere—he is conspicuously receptive to the forces around him. In and through this figure, these forces spring to life with unpredictable consequence, ready to abandon him or to take him along. Such are the whims of luck along the borderline.

Dropped onto the ground before the door to the hall of signs, the tailor, in his borderline existence, is momentarily cast in terms of consciousness and its loss. He "needed some time to come to his senses" (35), "Besinnung" (34). Before doing so, he is "more dead than alive" (35). The tailor in his near-death state has lost his sense, *Sinn*, in a variety of ways. In the literal range, a sensory rather than cognitive event has occurred at the point of entry into the underground. With his body on the earth, dermatic perceptions are prominently felt, if the tailor in this state feels anything at all. He is in the domain of the story, its sensibilities at the lines and membranes through which words resonate before signification.[29] He lies there suspended between life and death, just as he will find the woman in the coffin shortly, or rather immeasurably, thereafter.

The inklings of terror that surface with the woman's appearance emanate from a sleep akin to death. She loses her "consciousness" in an encounter with a stranger at whom she fires a bullet, which recoils from his chest into her horse's head and causes her to fall to the ground. With her body against the earth, she lies as the tailor did after his fall. In his state, at the membrane of senselessness and sense, loss of awareness and new life, a sensorily inflected consciousness emerged; in her condition, consciousness also encompasses a language beyond signification. The "several" words resounding in her ears as she lies on the ground are uttered, "murmured" (41), at the edge of silence. The stranger speaks these words, which remain unknown to us. Their effect is powerful, depriving her "of my consciousness" (41), "Bewußtsein" (40). Regaining her consciousness in the sensory zone in which it was lost, she "came to" her "senses," "kam" "zur Besinnung" (40), in the glass coffin. Consciousness returns with the very words that announce the tailor's revival. He, too, "comes" to his "Besinnung" (34). Conscious awareness in this coffin and on that ground before the door is linked more closely with sensory perception than with mentally distanced forms of knowledge. Different from "Besinnung," "Bewußtsein" resonates with "wissen," "to know."

In the underground of "The Glass Coffin," where the casket is lodged, a consciousness of the senses, *Besinnung*, makes itself heard. It is the voice of the story that speaks from such a consciousness. Like the voice from the wall, it is powerfully effective in its emotional consequence and allusive modulations. The consciousness permeated by knowledge, *Bewußtsein*, is associated with the machinery of the plot. The figure in the coffin, however, insists on her story, which draws upon—and searches for—*Besinnung*. The presentation of her story coincides with the awakening of her senses, a deeply affective *Besinnung*. Everything and everyone in "The Glass Coffin" is affected by the story that lurks underneath the plot, apparent now and then in inklings of terror and spurts of elation, at moments of precarious uncertainty and wonderment. As the story evolves, dreamlike sequences continue and dreaming itself comes to the fore. Consciousness surfaces in the vicinity of these manifestations, close to their affective oscillations and indeterminate edges.

The tailor, who is about to receive the story of the woman's "fate" ("Schicksals" [38]) through which she evolves as a primary protagonist, initially envisions the encased figure in an intensely undetermined moment. Instantly transported into an awareness beyond knowledge, he perceives her through his senses, arriving in the proximity of *Besinnung* once again.

For a brief interval, his consciousness had taken on the hardened, precisely defined shape of *Bewußtsein*. Immediately before the tailor casts his eyes onto the coffin behind his back, he is engaged in minutely detailed observations. In the glass case before him "everything was small, but made most carefully and delicately—carved, it seemed, with the greatest precision by an artful hand." The tailor's consciousness of the miniature buildings and delightful "things" (37), however, is not entirely subsumed by the highly determinate sights in the case. He is engaged in a contemplation of these objects that leaves room for a metaphorically inflected "artful hand." The range of the story, its metaphorical freedom, can be felt here.

An artful hand seems to have positioned the "most beautiful" figure in the coffin as well. She is "enveloped in long, blond hair as if in a precious cloak" (37). Her hair reminds the viewer of a garment, which it is not; attention is drawn to a barely covered body. A ribbon shifts back and forth, "moved" (37) by her breath. Tied to her hair perhaps, this ribbon indicates the subtle motion of her skin underneath. "With pounding heart" (37), the tailor gazes at the image, which then speaks, for a moment, from the depths of death. He is far away now from a consciousness allied with knowledge.

Speaking from the heart, he had been admitted to the hut of reeds and rushes. Perceiving with his eyes and heart, he is addressed by the figure behind glass. The encasement is permeated by speech; the walls of the hut had been penetrated by the noise outside in the morning. A dreamlike perception presses upon membranes and coverings throughout the tale, as if the story were about to sail off. If time stands still at the case, so does for a moment space shed its varied dimensions. A story before dispersion presents itself.

That story, the female protagonist's autobiographical account —which lies at the heart of the following chapter—intensifies the dreamlike atmosphere of the tale's fictional reality. At a most decisive moment, the tailor's journey, itself resembling a dream at times, arrives in her dream of release. Subjected to the incalculable workings of luck, his wanderings and adventures culminate in an event that has already taken place. Whatever has been left of fictional time, its progressive reality, dissolves through the lens of her dream. Shot through with lucky turns and catastrophic proximities, his experience eventually is incorporated into hers. Her "soul," "Seele" (40), perceives him before he knows. When his consciousness takes on a more sensual quality in front of the coffin, he begins to catch up with his story.

6

Between Dream and Wakefulness: The Female Protagonist in "The Glass Coffin"

> A breath of music or of a dream, of something that would make me almost feel, something that would make me not think.
>
> FERNANDO PESSOA
> *Livro do Desassossego*

Locked into her life against her will, the female protagonist in "The Glass Coffin" relates, but also reenacts a nightmarish silence. The events around the coffin are but the beginning of her revelations and conccalments. The skins and surfaces through which she appears for the tailor and for readers prefigure a drama at boundaries, the "story of my fate" (37). Silence, however, spreads in the midst of the love story. The tailor is rendered speechless as well. He will not utter another word for the rest of the tale. The new protagonist will tell her story, which emerges and—in insidious inversions—recedes incessantly. Enchantment is intertwined with transgression. A momentous past remains frozen, inaccessible to the words that reach out for it. A nightmarish feeling persists amorphously, never present in its full range. The female protagonist never quite emerges from a realm between dream and wakefulness, tormented memory and a life that might be possible beyond the confines of the glass coffin. The strange events in the midst of her castle trigger much turmoil and activity, but in the end a certain, if apparently happy, disengagement prevails. Notwithstanding an at times turbulent plot, not much, if anything of moment at all, has happened. Life here is all but tentative, remains on the verge of experience.

Fractured Enchantment

The female protagonist's narrative, which forms a distinct segment within "The Glass Coffin," speaks both in its detail and its omissions. The outlines of a fairy tale mark the beginning: the new protagonist belongs to a wealthy family; her parents die in her early childhood; her older brother brings her up; they love each other tenderly, resolve not to marry, and plan to stay with each other to the end of their lives.

This happy scenario is punctured in the course of one evening and night. The brother invites a stranger to spend some time at the castle. After some resistance, the stranger agrees to the proposal. An evening of conventional entertainment turns into a fateful night: barely asleep—the female protagonist recalls—she is awakened by tender sounds. Unable to ascertain their source, she attempts to call for help, but realizes she cannot utter a sound, "as if" in a "nightmare" (39).[30] In her paralyzed condition, she sees the stranger enter into her room, although its two doors are firmly locked.

Barely awake, the young woman finds herself in a nightmarish, dreamlike state brought about by "an unknown force" (39), which recalls the "mysterious force" (35) that had driven the tailor into the underground hall. If a story in the tale begins to speak here, it does so against a strikingly conventional background. The happy life the siblings envision leaves hardly any room for extraordinary experience, and the teller of the tale lacks a voice long before the stranger's arrival. She herself, as different from her brother, barely matters. The Last Wills of her parents give her brother authority over her. In a similar vein, she relates in her autobiographical account that her brother felt great "delight" in the stranger's "conversation and intermingled tales" (39). Her own feelings remain unspoken.

Offering very little memory of her parents, this protagonist defines herself in decidedly external terms as "the daughter of a rich count" (39). Having barely escaped the coffin, she erects another barrier between herself and the "poor" (33) tailor. Her status is part and parcel of the dominant tale in which the poor but lucky tailor wins the rich lady's hand and heart.

The lucky turns of the underlying story occur elsewhere. There the tailor does not achieve anything in established terms. On his way to the coffin—which appears before him surprisingly—he "abandoned himself to his fate" (35). Having done so on top of the horns, his path into the underground opens up, leading to the fateful encounter at the coffin. "It," "es" (32), works out luckily once he comes to his senses, "Besinnung" (34)—a consciousness beyond mere knowledge.

For this lucky traveler, "the daughter of a rich count" (39) does not spell good fortune. His story, and the story suppressed in his sister's account, speak in allusive modulations within the vocabulary offered in the tale. As words like "courage" and "luck" metamorphose at various points in the narrative, so does "fate."

The tailor who "abandoned himself to his fate" (35) is remembered in the "story of my fate" (37) presented by the female protagonist. At the onset of this remembrance, her account conflicts sharply with the story that led to her discovery. Although she has appeared at the tale's peripheries—in its linguistic underground, on the markings of its skin, in the oscillations of its emotional texture—she begins her narrative in a conventional middle ground. Yet the difference between the dominant tale and the underlying story reemerges in the wordings between the status-conscious opening and the merrymaking in the castle: "My parents died when I was still in my tender youth," the young woman relates, "and recommended me in their Last Wills to my older brother, by whom I was raised" (39). "Tender," vulnerable to injury, she is more fragile than the overall tale asserts. For this sensibility she receives little protection. Manheim's translation supplies the human element missing in the Wills by having her "entrusted" (510) to her brother.

The siblings, loving each other "tenderly" (39), live in a particular emotional atmosphere. The brother replaces the parents in a life of extraordinary, if not incestuous, closeness.[31] In the midst of the conventional happiness in the castle, a key element of the underlying story announces itself.

Beyond his love for his sister, the brother exhibits a pronounced sympathy for the stranger. In this instance, his feelings seem to differ from hers. Not just a conversationalist, the stranger also is a storyteller. His "tales" (39) enter into "The Glass Coffin," as signs of her story are beginning to puncture the ostensibly cheerful proceedings in the castle. While these tales remain unwritten, they nevertheless resonate in the reactions of the siblings. In an environment, furthermore, where "conversation" (39) would take a conventional course, such tales are comparatively unfettered. If heard at the periphery of conversational etiquette, the stranger's tales connect with the concealed narrative in "The Glass Coffin." In this potential space, the stranger and the story, her story, are beginning to interact.[32] It is the sister who is telling the story that highlights the stranger's hesitation to spend the night at the castle and her brother's insistence on his continued presence. It appears that she is beginning to see the stranger, as well as her brother, through her own eyes.

In Wilhelm Grimm's earlier presentation of this passage in a journal,[33] the tales related by the stranger and his conversational skills leave markedly different impressions in the familial pair. While the brother's pronounced sympathy for the stranger in the later printing barely hints at a rift between the siblings, the preceding version has the sister tell that in the midst of his talking the stranger "looked at me many a time with fiery and penetrating eyes."[34] The next sentence speaks of the brother's great "delight" (39) with the visitor. Incestuously inflected, this pleasure resonates with the stranger's transgressive entry[35] into the sister's bedroom—"he himself," she hears from the stranger, "was penetrating through all the locks with the intention of offering me his heart and hand" (39).

Dream and reality—if they still can be distinguished from each other as such—now enter more visibly into strange interactions. Imagined from the sister's perspective, already the entertainment in the castle had appeared as if behind glass, with her feelings encased. The sleep she finds at the end of the very long evening is light, and once awake again, the stranger and the nightmarish loss of her voice he causes occupy the consciousness she seems to have attained. As she is lying on her bed as if in a coffin, her future state is prefigured.

Signs of Transgression

At every turn of the tale, the story now speaks. In the account of the merry life in the castle, the surface plot had dominated, with cracks apparent only toward the end. In the night of and with the stranger, the story comes to the fore.

Tired as the sister is, she rushes "to rest my limbs on my soft feather bed" (39). It is a familiar scene. At the onset of his journey, the tailor—fearing wild beasts—had foregone laying down on the "good bed" (33). For a short while, his female counterpart finds the kind of resting place that eluded him. The contours of her body and the skin through which she later communicates with him from the coffin are received by her "soft" bed. In its downy material, the beasts that threatened the tailor are opaquely remembered and transformed. The birds, who thus contribute to her rest, belong to her story. They recall the tailor's airy experience at edges of possibility and disaster. Perched on the treetop, his little body compressed and spread out, the tailor had metamorphosed into a wing-like form. On top of the horns, he had sailed through the air, at risk of being dropped anywhere at any time.

As the young woman is lying in her bed, the events and eventualities that gripped him begin to resound in her slumber. Aroused by "tender and lovely" (39) music, she crosses a line back into wakefulness, and shortly thereafter into a nightmarish zone. In the music, words of the story resurface in telling modulations. The "tender" sounds recall her "tender" (39), fragile youth and the love the siblings gave to each other "so tenderly" (39).

"Lovely" as it is, the music further activates the woman's emotional past and present. Nowhere do we hear of parental love: "We loved each other" (39) refers to the siblings. The tailor, as she says immediately before her narrative, shall spend his life "loved by me and showered with every earthly possession" (37). Both the love of the past couple, with the custodial brother in charge, and that between the tailor and the maiden suggests a transgressive thrust.

Conspicuously silent in the wake of his discovery in the glass coffin, the tailor is presented with the conditions of the rest of his life. The words put to him by his self-announced bride leave no room for activities, let alone dreams of his own. Everything is taken care of for him. In terms of the tale, he is lucky indeed. In the context of the underlying story, he is caught in the operations of the forge. Luck has hardened in his bride's announcement: it is tightly linked with his destiny, part and parcel of "the story of my fate" (37) as told by the female protagonist.

Is this narration then after all merely the tale of her fate? If the maiden's past and the tailor's future were to spread out seamlessly and clearly before them, the story would be buried once and for all. But as her narrative unfolds, it is torn back and forth between clearness and obscurity, between an outright happy plot and diffuse, enigmatic undertones. The story speaks, but it does not provide definite wordings. From the tale's beginning, elements of the story engage linguistic potentialities and appeal to a poetically energized imagination. As the maiden's announced narrative develops toward her story, such an imagination appears but tentatively—in muted, even silenced form.

Suspended on the way to her story, the female protagonist moves about between dream and reality. As we hear the "tender and lovely" (39) music, longings and torments merge without resolution. Whereas the tailor had been invigorated by a voice associated with a "mysterious force" (35), the "unknown force" (39) to which the woman is subjected takes language away from her. In her the tailor does not solely find further resonances of his story, but also a deep-seated feeling of resistance, even blockage: like him, she does not have access to the consciousness called *Bewußtsein*.

Yet the woman's story, unlike the tailor's, is not permeated by enchanting manifestations of the more sensory consciousness that appears in "The Glass Coffin" as *Besinnung*. A nightmarish awareness envelops her in which her senses are subjected to intense pressures, with the stranger offering her his "heart and hand" (39). This proposition is not a gentle one—the stranger enters her room against her will and casts a spell on her ability to make sense out of her life, to attain *Besinnung*. As he generates the "tender and lovely" (39) music, in which the longings and the turmoil of her former life resonate, she loses her voice.

The stranger, it appears, confronts the female protagonist with her story and with a silence in its midst. He enters "by the light"— "shine," "Schein" (38)—"of the night lamp" (39), which recalls the uncertainties at the door to the old man's hut. From that door the tailor had found his way into the underground and to the coffin. The two locked doors through which the woman sees the stranger enter into her room connect with the opening to the hut as the tailor's story does to hers throughout. Again the female figure's narrative plunges into an enigmatic depth. Traces of the old man, a figure of the heart and of eclectic marginality, appear in the two doors.

Perceived in sensory suspension between dream and wakefulness, these doors furthermore conjure up the parental couple. If these parents left a legacy of transgressive love—to be felt around the brother figure empowered in their last wills—the tightly locked doors have been open for a very long time. There is no hiding in the castle. As walls, locks, generational boundaries, and familial taboos dissolve, the story presses upon the tale, which in spite of the drama that continues to dominate the plot now recedes into the background.

In the course of only eight sentences, the brother vanishes, a servant's horse collapses, the stranger appears with a stag—the transformed brother—on a leash, and the female protagonist fires a shot at the stranger, which bounces back into her horse's head, throwing her to the ground, where some murmured words uttered by the stranger make her lose her consciousness. In presenting these and the preceding events with increasing alacrity, even breathlessness, the protagonist reproduces the calamities that befell her. She also turns into the narrator of her story in spite of the outward tale's boisterous machinations. With one event chasing the other in a cataclysm of facticity, the tale's foreground developments turn hollow.

Linguistic modulations further amplify the transgressive pressure on boundaries. The stranger arrives in the "Schloß" (38), "castle," and later forces his way through all "Schlösser" (38), "locks." In dreamlike condensations the woman's story speaks from an evocative cluster of words and images. Someone and something, moving through the doors and walls as if they did not exist, arrives at this most porous moment in the story, reentering from a long time ago when someone was very small, a mere something, an "it," "es" (32), like the tailor at the beginning.

The permeability of the locks as well as the cold force associated with them and the castle are further prefigured in the door to the underground, which is pushed open with brute "force," "Gewalt" (34), by the very antlers the tailor rode at the risk of being pierced. That push enables the tailor to enter into the woman's underground world, which is turning out to be dominated by transgressions at and across primary boundaries. The walls and doors here, which do not provide enclosures for the female protagonist, do not stand and fall in isolation.

Liminal Inversions

The language of the skin, which speaks at every decisive turn—at the coffin, around the treetop, on top of the horns, in the underground hall—underlies the walls, doors, and locks everywhere. The stronger their initial appearance, the weaker the protective power of the walls and locks proves to be—and vice versa. The little hut of reeds and rushes provides the enclosure and resting point from which the story evolves. This hut is vulnerable and utterly necessary for "it," the cryptic story, to continue. The hut protects the ground on which the tailor finds a "rather good place to sleep" (35), which echoes the soft moss that would have been "a good bed" (33) and anticipates the ground in front of the rock wall from which his awareness will arise out of a most rudimentary uncertainty. The tailor and the ground are almost one: his body and mind, "more dead than alive" (35), follow the contours of the earth. Before his life begins to come forth again in a more differentiated form, it stirs along these contiguous surfaces, as the maiden's life does in the skin embedded within the coffin.

In and through thin skins—touched by death at times—the story finds its way back into the tale, remaining alive in spite of a dramatic plot. The effects of this plot recede before the affect of the story whenever the latter makes itself seen and heard. If the story then does not have the last word, it speaks in silence, at borderlines between language and speechlessness. When this silence spreads into the tale, words and sentences enter into states of confusion. They lose their territorial power, their ability to mark and define spots and spaces. In this uncertainty, the protagonists and the figures around them are within the reach of forces beyond control, and of death. Deep-seated anxieties lurk at these edges, among them the fear of dissolution, of losing one's skin irretrievably. The tailor on the ground and the lady in the coffin live and communicate at and through their physical peripheries. There is nothing beyond that to speak of.

Fears of being torn to pieces, shredded, or exposed crystallize at the protagonists' skins. The lady in the coffin lies as if on exhibition, and hurries for cover once the enclosure made of glass has been opened. But in her story the dreadful theme recurs. Through the stranger the walls and locks of her room and castle open up, no longer providing her with a space for sleep. From then on she lives between dream and wakefulness, neither knowing nor sensing where she might find one or the other. Everything is transparent and fluid.

The female protagonist's fate, which she tries to put into words, and her luck, which is intimately tied to the tailor's, are drawn into ever-recurring contingencies. In the course of her story, the lucky turn, through which the tailor discovers her beauty and their future lives in the case behind him, becomes virtually indistinguishable from the nightmarish pressures on her sense of reality and her individual consciousness. The emotional fluidity and freshness of the first experience at the coffin turns out to be closely akin to the torrent of events and the painful twists in her story of fractured enchantment. In the uncertain light, the *Schein* of this story, the scene of love at the coffin is punctured by moments of terror, from whose reign that pivotal occasion springs much like the bullet from the stranger's chest.

Yet it is the woman herself who has fired this projectile, which sends her to the ground toward the stranger's murmured words before she falls into the unconsciousness from which she awakes in the coffin. The stranger in this sequence is her vehicle, a "monster" (41) that does not fire a shot; she does it herself in her "most intense rage" (41), which is triggered by the realization—or the dream—that the stranger has transformed her brother into the stag on his leash. Yet the brother is strongly linked to the "lovely" and "tender" (39) transgressions the sister perceives to issue from the stranger.

The tailor, designated to be her future husband, seems to be excepted from this melee of intertwined identities. Yet undertones of the sister's account cast doubt on his singular status. The tailor rides toward the underground, and her coffin, on top of the horns that prove to be her brother's. Plucked from the ground against his will, rushed toward an unknown destination at breakneck speed, and dropped onto the ground in a daze, the tailor turns into an object of brotherly intensity. In the wake of this ride, the tailor finds the female protagonist, an event that seems to mark a new phase in the woman's life, beyond her incestuous ties to her family. Yet her brother remains forcefully present. Having delivered the tailor to her immediate vicinity, he resurfaces at the wedding in the same last sentence of the tale and story in which the union between the two protagonists is announced:

> Her joy increased even more when her brother, who had killed the magician in the form of the bull, came out of the forest in human shape; and on the very same day the maiden, following her promise, gave the happy tailor her hand at the altar. (41, 43)

As the lady marries the tailor, her brother rejoins her. The siblings' earlier resolve to stay together for the rest of their lives returns as she enters into marital union. To be sure, her "promise," "Versprechen" (42), to the tailor is thus fulfilled. In keeping her word, the uncertainties of her life seem to lie behind her at last. Yet "Versprechen," with its connotation of slip of the tongue, tells the old story. Although she lives up to her promise in the tale, she slips back into the underlying narrative in this deceptively "happy" ending. Her "joy" at the sight of her brother resonates with the terror in her room and at the coffin. Her brother's presence in her new marriage brings their family back into the narrative at its moment of apparent closure: the case of glass stands ready to open and shut again.

By recalling various elements of the narrative, the tale once more resounds with the story. The old beginning is only a nightmare away. Although the tale at the moment of marriage presents a "glücklichen" (42)—"happy," with an undertone of good luck—tailor, the question remains whether "it," "es" (32), turned out luckily for him. In their intricate interaction, the lucky outcome and the slippery promise amplify the tale's instability at its end. The *Versprechen* whose fulfillment renders the tailor lucky also reactivates the unpredictable forces of his journey. "It" continues to undermine the desire to forge luck into definite, reliable shapes. Luck evaporates through a slip of the tongue, while the promise, "Versprechen" (42), is in turn subjected to an irreducibly elusive fortune. The tale's first sentence, which inaugurates a story of luck attaching to no one in particular, reverberates in the last.

7

Brüder Grimm
Der treue Johannes[36]

Es war einmal ein alter König, der war krank und dachte 'es wird wohl das Todtenbett sein, auf dem ich liege.' Da sprach er 'laßt mir den getreuen Johannes kommen.' Der getreue Johannes war sein liebster Diener, und hieß so, weil er ihm sein Lebelang so treu gewesen war. Als er nun vor das Bett kam, sprach der König zu ihm 'getreuester Johannes, ich fühle daß mein Ende heran naht, und da habe ich keine andere Sorge als um meinen Sohn: er ist noch in jungen Jahren, wo er sich nicht immer zu rathen weiß, und wenn du mir nicht versprichst ihn zu unterrichten in allem, was er wissen muß, und sein Pflegevater zu sein, so kann ich meine Augen nicht in Ruhe schließen.' Da antwortete der getreue Johannes 'ich will ihn nicht verlassen, und will ihm mit Treue dienen, wenns auch mein Leben kostet.' Da sagte der alte König 'so sterb ich getrost und in Frieden.' Und sprach dann weiter 'nach meinem Tode sollst du ihm das ganze Schloß zeigen, alle Kammern, Säle und Gewölbe, und alle Schätze, die darin liegen: aber die letzte Kammer in dem langen Gange sollst du ihm nicht zeigen, worin das Bild der Königstochter vom goldenen Dache verborgen steht. Wenn er das Bild erblickt, wird er eine heftige Liebe zu ihr empfinden, und wird in Ohnmacht niederfallen und wird ihretwegen in große Gefahren gerathen; davor sollst du ihn hüten.' Und als der treue Johannes nochmals dem alten König die Hand darauf gegeben hatte, ward dieser still, legte sein Haupt auf das Kissen und starb.

Als der alte König zu Grabe getragen war, da erzählte der treue Johannes dem jungen König was er seinem Vater auf dem Sterbelager versprochen hatte, und sagte 'das will ich gewißlich halten, und will dir treu sein, wie ich ihm gewesen bin, und sollte es mein Leben kosten.' Die Trauer gieng vorüber, da sprach der treue Johannes zu ihm 'es ist nun Zeit, daß du dein Erbe siehst: ich will dir dein väterliches Schloß zeigen.' Da führte er ihn überall herum, auf und ab, und ließ ihn alle die Reichthümer und prächtigen Kammern sehen: nur die eine Kammer öffnete er nicht, worin das gefährliche

Faithful Johannes

*O*nce there was an old king who was ill and thought: "It appears I am lying on my deathbed." Then he said: "Have Faithful Johannes come to me." Faithful Johannes was his favorite servant, and was so called because all of his life he had been so faithful to him. When he now came to the bedside, the king said to him: "Most faithful Johannes, I feel that my end is approaching, and now I have no worry except about my son: he is still young and does not always know how to go about his life, and if you don't promise me to educate him in everything he needs to know and to be his foster father, I will not be able to close my eyes in peace." Then Faithful Johannes replied: "I will not abandon him and will serve him faithfully, even if it costs me my life." Thereupon the old king said: "Now I can depart in comfort and peace." And then he continued: "Following my death you are to show him the whole castle, all the chambers, halls, and vaults, and all the treasures that are in them; but you are not to show him the last chamber in the long corridor, in which the likeness of the Princess of the Golden Roof is hidden. If he catches sight of that likeness, he will feel passionate love for her and fall down in a faint, and he will encounter great perils because of her; from that you are to protect him." And when Faithful Johannes had once more assured the old king that he would carry out his promise, the king fell silent, laid his head on his pillow, and died.

Once the old king had been borne to his grave, Faithful Johannes told the young king what he had promised his father on his deathbed, and said: "That promise I certainly intend to keep and I will be as faithful to you as I was to him, even if it should cost me my life." The time of mourning had passed, and now Faithful Johannes said to the king: "It is now time for you to see your inheritance: I want to show you your father's castle." Then he led him around everywhere, upstairs and down, and let him see all the riches and splendid chambers: only the one chamber, in which there was the dangerous

Bild stand. Das Bild war aber so gestellt, daß, wenn die Thüre aufgieng, man gerade darauf sah, und war so herrlich gemacht, daß man meinte es leibte und lebte, und es gäbe nichts lieblicheres und schöneres auf der ganzen Welt. Der junge König aber merkte wohl daß der getreue Johannes immer an einer Thür vorübergieng und sprach 'warum schließest du mir diese niemals auf?' 'Es ist etwas darin,' antwortete er, 'vor dem du erschrickst.' Aber der König antwortete 'ich habe das ganze Schloß gesehen, so will ich auch wissen was darin ist,' gieng und wollte die Thüre mit Gewalt öffnen. Da hielt ihn der getreue Johannes zurück und sagte 'ich habe es deinem Vater vor seinem Tode versprochen, daß du nicht sehen sollst was in der Kammer steht: es könnte dir und mir zu großem Unglück ausschlagen.' 'Ach nein,' antwortete der junge König, wenn ich nicht hineinkomme, so ists mein sicheres Verderben: ich würde Tag und Nacht keine Ruhe haben, bis ichs mit meinen Augen gesehen hätte. Nun gehe ich nicht von der Stelle, bis du aufgeschlossen hast.'

Da sah der getreue Johannes daß es nicht mehr zu ändern war, und suchte mit schwerem Herzen und vielem Seufzen aus dem großen Bund den Schlüssel heraus. Als er die Thüre geöffnet hatte, trat er zuerst hinein und dachte er wolle das Bildnis bedecken daß es der König vor ihm nicht sähe: aber was half das? der König stellte sich auf die Fußspitzen und sah ihm über die Schulter. Und als er das Bildnis der Jungfrau erblickte, das so herrlich war und von Gold und Edelsteinen glänzte, da fiel er ohnmächtig zur Erde nieder. Der getreue Johannes hob ihn auf, trug ihn in sein Bett und dachte voll Sorgen 'das Unglück ist geschehen, Herr Gott, was will daraus werden!' dann stärkte er ihn mit Wein, bis er wieder zu sich selbst kam. Das erste Wort, das er sprach, war 'ach! wer ist das schöne Bild?' 'Das ist die Königstochter vom goldenen Dache,' antwortete der treue Johannes. Da sprach der König weiter 'meine Liebe zu ihr ist so groß, wenn alle Blätter an den Bäumen Zungen wären, sie könntens nicht aussagen; mein Leben setze ich daran, daß ich sie erlange. Du bist mein getreuster Johannes, du mußt mir beistehen.'

Der treue Diener besann sich lange wie die Sache anzufangen wäre, denn es hielt schwer, nur vor das Angesicht der Königstochter zu kommen. Endlich hatte er ein Mittel ausgedacht und sprach zu dem König 'alles, was sie um sich hat, ist von Gold, Tische, Stühle, Schüsseln, Becher, Näpfe und alles Hausgeräth: in deinem Schatze liegen fünf Tonnen Goldes, laß eine von den Goldschmieden des Reichs verarbeiten zu allerhand Gefäßen und Geräthschaften, zu allerhand Vögeln, Gewild und wunderbaren Thieren, das wird

likeness, he did not open. Now, the likeness was placed in such a way that once the door was opened one looked straight at it, and it was so magnificently composed that one thought it breathed and lived and that there was nothing more lovely and more beautiful in the whole world. The young king, however, certainly noticed that Faithful Johannes always walked past one particular door, and he said: "Why don't you ever unlock that one for me?" "There is something in there," he replied, "that would frighten you." But the king answered, "I have seen the whole castle, and so I also want to know what is in there," and he went and wanted to open the door by force. But Faithful Johannes held him back and said: "I promised your father before his death that you would not be allowed to see what is in that chamber: this could spell great misfortune for you and me." "Ah, no," replied the young king, "if I do not get in, it will be my certain ruin: I would have no rest day or night until I had seen it with my own eyes. Now I will not move from this place until you have unlocked that door."

Thus Faithful Johannes saw that he could do nothing about it any more, and with a heavy heart and much sighing, he picked the key out of the big bunch. When he had opened the door, he went in first and thought he would thus cover the likeness so that the king would not see it in front of him; but what was the good of that? The king stood on the tips of his toes and looked over his shoulder. And when he caught sight of the maiden's likeness, which was so magnificent and glittered with gold and precious stones, he fell to the ground in a faint. Faithful Johannes lifted him up, carried him to his bed, and thought with great sorrow: "The misfortune has arrived, Good Lord, what will come of this?" Then he reinvigorated him with some wine, until he was himself again. The first words he spoke were: "Ah, who is that beautiful likeness?" "That is the Princess of the Golden Roof," replied Faithful Johannes. And the king continued: "My love for her is so great that if all the leaves on the trees were tongues they could not express it; I will risk my life to win her. You are my most faithful Johannes, you must help me."

The faithful servant considered for a long time how to go about this matter, for it was difficult even to meet the princess face-to-face. At last he thought of a way, and said to the king: "Everything she has around her is made of gold: tables, chairs, bowls, goblets, dishes, and all the household utensils. There are five tons of gold in your treasury; from one of them, have the goldsmiths of your kingdom manufacture all kinds of vessels and utensils, and all kinds of birds, wild animals, and marvelous creatures: that will

ihr gefallen, wir wollen damit hinfahren und unser Glück versuchen.' Der König hieß alle Goldschmiede herbei holen, die mußten Tag und Nacht arbeiten, bis endlich die herrlichsten Dinge fertig waren. Als alles auf ein Schiff geladen war, zog der getreue Johannes Kaufmannskleider an, und der König mußte ein gleiches thun, um sich ganz unkenntlich zu machen. Dann fuhren sie über das Meer, und fuhren so lange, bis sie zu der Stadt kamen, worin die Königstochter vom goldenen Dache wohnte.

Der treue Johannes hieß den König auf dem Schiffe zurückbleiben und auf ihn warten. *'Vielleicht,'* sprach er, *'bring ich die Königstochter mit, darum sorgt daß alles in Ordnung ist, laßt die Goldgefäße aufstellen und das ganze Schiff ausschmücken.'* Darauf suchte er sich in sein Schürzchen allerlei von den Goldsachen zusammen, stieg ans Land und gieng gerade nach dem königlichen Schloß. Als er in den Schloßhof kam, stand da beim Brunnen ein schönes Mädchen, das hatte zwei goldene Eimer in der Hand und schöpfte damit. Und als es das blinkende Wasser forttragen wollte und sich umdrehte, sah es den fremden Mann und fragte wer er wäre? Da antwortete er *'ich bin ein Kaufmann,'* und öffnete sein Schürzchen und ließ sie hineinschauen. Da rief sie *'ei, was für schönes Goldzeug!'* setzte die Eimer nieder und betrachtete eins nach dem andern. Da sprach das Mädchen *'das muß die Königstochter sehen, die hat so große Freude an den Goldsachen, daß sie euch alles abkauft.'* Es nahm ihn bei der Hand und führte ihn hinauf, denn es war die Kammerjungfer. Als die Königstochter die Waare sah, war sie ganz vergnügt und sprach *'es ist so schön gearbeitet, daß ich dir alles abkaufen will.'* Aber der getreue Johannes sprach *'ich bin nur der Diener von einem reichen Kaufmann: was ich hier habe ist nichts gegen das, was mein Herr auf seinem Schiff stehen hat, und das ist das künstlichste und köstlichste, was je in Gold ist gearbeitet worden.'* Sie wollte alles herauf gebracht haben, aber er sprach *'dazu gehören viele Tage, so groß ist die Menge, und so viel Säle um es aufzustellen, daß euer Haus nicht Raum dafür hat.'* Da ward ihre Neugierde und Lust immer mehr angeregt, so daß sie endlich sagte *'führe mich hin zu dem Schiff, ich will selbst hingehen und deines Herrn Schätze betrachten.'*

Da führte sie der getreue Johannes zu dem Schiffe hin und war ganz freudig, und der König, als er sie erblickte, sah daß ihre Schönheit noch größer war, als das Bild sie dargestellt hatte, und meinte nicht anders als das Herz wollte ihm zerspringen. Nun stieg sie in das Schiff, und der König führte sie hinein; der getreue Johannes aber blieb zurück bei dem Steuermann

please her, we will journey there with those things and try our luck." The king summoned all the goldsmiths, and they had to work day and night until at last the most magnificent things were ready. When everything had been loaded on board a ship, Faithful Johannes put on merchant's clothes, and the king had to do the same in order to make himself entirely unrecognizable. Then they sailed across the sea and kept sailing until they came to the city where the Princess of the Golden Roof lived.

Faithful Johannes told the king to remain on the ship and to wait for him. *"Perhaps,"* he said, *"I will bring the princess back with me, therefore take care that all is in order, have the golden vessels set out and the whole ship decorated."* Then he gathered all kinds of golden things into his apron, went ashore, and walked straight to the royal castle. When he entered the courtyard, a beautiful girl was standing there by the fountain, and she had two golden buckets in her hands, drawing water with them. And when she wanted to carry away the glistening water and turned around, she saw the stranger and asked who he was. And he answered: *"I am a merchant,"* and opened his apron and let her look in. And she exclaimed: *"Ah, what beautiful golden things!"* and put her buckets down, and looked at the golden wares one by one. Then the girl said: *"The princess must see these, she so much enjoys golden things that she will buy everything from you."* She took him by the hand and led him in, for she was the lady's maid. When the princess saw the wares, she was most pleased and said: *"They are so beautifully made that I wish to buy them all."* But Faithful Johannes said: *"I am only the servant of a rich merchant; what I have here is nothing compared to what my master has on his ship: the most artful and delightful things ever made of gold."* She wanted everything brought up to her, but he said: *"There is so much that in order to do this one would need many days and so many halls for exhibiting everything that your house would not have enough space for it."* This excited her curiosity and desire more and more, so that at last she said: *"Take me to the ship, I want to go there myself and view your master's treasures."*

So Faithful Johannes led her to the ship, and he felt very joyful, and the king, when he caught sight of her, saw that her beauty was even greater than represented in the likeness, and he thought that surely his heart would burst. Now she stepped on board, and the king led her inside the ship; Faithful Johannes, however, stayed behind with the helmsman and ordered the ship to be pushed off: *"Set all sails to make it fly like a bird in the air."* And the king

und hieß das Schiff abstoßen, 'spannt alle Segel auf, daß es fliegt wie ein Vogel in der Luft.' Der König aber zeigte ihr drinnen das goldene Geschirr, jedes einzeln, die Schüsseln, Becher, Näpfe, die Vögel, das Gewild und die wunderbaren Thiere. Viele Stunden giengen herum, während sie alles besah, und in ihrer Freude merkte sie nicht daß das Schiff dahin fuhr. Nachdem sie das letzte betrachtet hatte, dankte sie dem Kaufmann und wollte heim, als sie aber an des Schiffes Rand kam, sah sie daß es fern vom Land auf hohem Meere gieng und mit vollen Segeln forteilte. 'Ach,' rief sie erschrocken, 'ich bin betrogen, ich bin entführt und in die Gewalt eines Kaufmanns gerathen; lieber wollt ich sterben!' Der König aber faßte sie bei der Hand und sprach 'ein Kaufmann bin ich nicht, ich bin ein König und nicht geringer an Geburt als du bist: aber daß ich dich mit List entführt habe, das ist aus übergroßer Liebe geschehen. Das erstemal, als ich dein Bildnis gesehen habe, bin ich ohnmächtig zur Erde gefallen.' Als die Königstochter vom goldenen Dache das hörte, ward sie getröstet, und ihr Herz ward ihm geneigt, so daß sie gerne einwilligte seine Gemahlin zu werden.

Es trug sich aber zu, während sie auf dem hohen Meere dahin fuhren, daß der getreue Johannes, als er vorn auf dem Schiffe saß und Musik machte, in der Luft drei Raben erblickte, die daher geflogen kamen. Da hörte er auf zu spielen und horchte was sie mit einander sprachen, denn er verstand das wohl. Die eine rief 'ei, da führt er die Königstochter vom goldenen Dache heim.' 'Ja,' antwortete die zweite, 'er hat sie noch nicht.' Sprach die dritte 'er hat sie doch, sie sitzt bei ihm im Schiffe.' Da fieng die erste wieder an und rief 'was hilft ihm das! wenn sie ans Land kommen, wird ihm ein fuchsrothes Pferd entgegenspringen: da wird er sich aufschwingen wollen, und thut er das, so sprengt es mit ihm fort und in die Luft hinein, daß er nimmer mehr seine Jungfrau wieder sieht.' Sprach die zweite 'ist gar keine Rettung?' 'O ja, wenn ein anderer schnell aufsitzt, das Feuergewehr, das in den Halftern stecken muß, heraus nimmt und das Pferd damit todt schießt, so ist der junge König gerettet. Aber wer weiß das! und wers weiß und sagts ihm, der wird zu Stein von den Fußzehen bis zum Knie.' Da sprach die zweite 'ich weiß noch mehr, wenn das Pferd auch getödtet wird, so behält der junge König doch nicht seine Braut: wenn sie zusammen ins Schloß kommen, so liegt dort ein gemachtes Brauthemd in einer Schüssel, und sieht aus als wärs von Gold und Silber gewebt, ist aber nichts als Schwefel und Pech: wenn ers anthut, verbrennt es ihn bis aufs Mark und Knochen.' Sprach die dritte 'ist

showed her the golden wares inside, every one of them, the bowls, goblets, dishes, and the birds, the wild animals, and the marvelous creatures. Many hours went by while she looked at everything, and in her joy she did not notice that the ship was sailing along. After she had viewed the last piece, she thanked the merchant and wanted to go home, but when she reached the side of the ship she saw that it was on the high seas far from the shore and that it was rushing onward under full sail. "Ah," she exclaimed in fright, "I have been betrayed and kidnapped, and I have fallen into the hands of a merchant; I would rather die!" But the king took her by the hand and said: "I am not a merchant: I am a king and no less by birth than you are; but if I have carried you off with cunning, that happened because of my overwhelming love. The first time I saw your likeness, I fell to the ground in a faint." When the Princess of the Golden Roof heard that, she felt reassured, and her heart opened up for him, so that she gladly consented to become his wife.

While they were sailing along on the high seas, however, it came to pass that Faithful Johannes, as he was sitting and playing music in the bow of the ship, caught sight of three ravens in the air, who came flying towards them. So he stopped playing and listened to what they were saying to each other, for he understood that well. One exclaimed: "Ah, there he is, taking home the Princess of the Golden Roof." "Yes," the second responded, "he does not have her yet." Said the third: "He does have her, she is sitting beside him in the ship." Then the first began again, and exclaimed: "What good will that do him! When they reach land, a fox-colored, red horse will leap towards him; so he will want to mount it, and if he does that, it will gallop off with him, up into the air, so that he will never again see his maiden." Said the second: "Is there no remedy at all?" "Oh yes, if someone else jumps on it quickly, takes out the gun, which will be in its holster, and with that shoots the horse dead, the young king will be saved. But who would know that! And whoever knows that and tells him, will turn to stone from his toes to his knees." Then the second said: "I know still more—even if the horse is killed, the young king will still not keep his bride; when they come into the castle together, a wrought bridal robe will be lying there in a bowl, looking as if woven of gold and silver, but it is nothing but sulphur and pitch: if he puts it on, it will burn him to the marrow of his bones." Said the third: "Is there no remedy at all?" "Oh yes," the second responded, "if someone seizes the robe with gloves and tosses it into the fire, so that it burns up, the young king will be saved. But what good will that do! Whoever knows that and tells him will have half

da gar keine Rettung?' 'O ja,' antwortete die zweite, 'wenn einer mit Handschuhen das Hemd packt und wirft es ins Feuer, daß es verbrennt, so ist der junge König gerettet. Aber was hilfts! wers weiß und es ihm sagt, der wird halbes Leibes Stein vom Knie bis zum Herzen.' Da sprach die dritte 'ich weiß noch mehr, wird das Brauthemd auch verbrannt, so hat der junge König seine Braut doch noch nicht: wenn nach der Hochzeit der Tanz anhebt, und die junge Königin tanzt, wird sie plötzlich erbleichen und wie todt hinfallen: und hebt sie nicht einer auf und zieht aus ihrer rechten Brust drei Tropfen Blut und speit sie wieder aus, so stirbt sie. Aber verräth das einer, der es weiß, so wird er ganzes Leibes zu Stein vom Wirbel bis zur Fußzehe.' Als die Raben das mit einander gesprochen hatten, flogen sie weiter, und der getreue Johannes hatte alles wohl verstanden, aber von der Zeit an war er still und traurig; denn verschwieg er seinem Herrn, was er gehört hatte, so war dieser unglücklich: entdeckte er es ihm, so mußte er selbst sein Leben hingeben. Endlich aber sprach er bei sich 'meinen Herrn will ich retten, und sollt ich selbst darüber zu Grunde gehen.'

Als sie nun ans Land kamen, da geschah es, wie die Rabe vorher gesagt hatte, und es sprengte ein prächtiger fuchsrother Gaul daher. 'Wohlan,' sprach der König, 'der soll mich in mein Schloß tragen,' und wollte sich aufsetzen, doch der treue Johannes kam ihm zuvor, schwang sich schnell darauf, zog das Gewehr aus den Halftern, und schoß den Gaul nieder. Da riefen die andern Diener des Königs, die dem treuen Johannes doch nicht gut waren, 'wie schändlich, das schöne Thier zu tödten, das den König in sein Schloß tragen sollte!' Aber der König sprach 'schweigt und laßt ihn gehen, es ist mein getreuester Johannes, wer weiß wozu das gut ist!' Nun giengen sie ins Schloß, und da stand im Saal eine Schüssel, und das gemachte Brauthemd lag darin und sah aus nicht anders als wäre es von Gold und Silber. Der junge König gieng darauf zu und wollte es ergreifen, aber der treue Johannes schob ihn weg, packte es mit Handschuhen an, trug es schnell ins Feuer und ließ es verbrennen. Die anderen Diener fiengen wieder an zu murren und sagten 'seht, nun verbrennt er gar des Königs Brauthemd.' Aber der junge König sprach 'wer weiß wozu es gut ist, laßt ihn gehen, es ist mein getreuester Johannes.' Nun ward die Hochzeit gefeiert: der Tanz hub an, und die Braut trat auch hinein, da hatte der treue Johannes Acht und schaute ihr ins Antlitz; auf einmal erbleichte sie und fiel wie todt zur Erde. Da sprang er eilends hinzu, hob sie auf und trug sie in eine Kammer, da legte er sie nieder,

Faithful Johannes   81

of his body turned to stone, from his knees to his heart." Then the third said: "I know still more—even if the bridal robe is burned, the young king will still not have his bride; when the dancing begins after the wedding, and the young queen dances, she will suddenly turn pale and fall down as if dead: and unless someone lifts her up and draws three drops of blood from her right breast, and spits them out, she will die. But if someone who knows that were to give it away, his entire body would be turned to stone, from the top of his spine to his toes." After the ravens had thus talked with each other, they flew on; and Faithful Johannes had understood everything well, but from that time on he was quiet and sad; for if he kept what he had heard from his master, the latter would suffer misfortune, and if he revealed it to him, he himself would have to give his life. But at last he said to himself: "I want to save my master, even if that brings about my end."

    Now, when they reached land, what the raven had foretold did happen, and a splendid, fox-colored, red horse came galloping toward them. "Well," the king said, "that one shall carry me to my castle," and he wanted to mount it, but Faithful Johannes was faster than him, quickly mounted it, drew the gun out of its holster, and shot the horse. At that the king's other servants, who after all were not fond of Faithful Johannes, exclaimed: "What a shame to kill the beautiful creature, which was to carry the king to his castle!" But the king said: "Be silent and let him go, he is my most faithful Johannes, who knows what good may come of that!" Now they went into the castle, and there, in the hall, stood a bowl, and the wrought bridal robe lay in it and looked exactly as if it were made of gold and silver. The young king went toward it and wanted to take hold of it, but Faithful Johannes shoved him aside, seized it with gloves, carried it quickly to the fire and let it burn. The other servants began to grumble again and said: "Look, now he is even burning the king's bridal robe." But the young king said: "Who knows what good may come of that, let him go, he is my most faithful Johannes." Now the wedding was celebrated: the dancing began, and the bride took part in it as well, and so Faithful Johannes was alert and looked at her face; suddenly she turned pale and fell to the ground as if dead. At that he quickly ran to her, lifted her up and carried her into a chamber; there he laid her down, knelt beside her, and sucked the three drops of blood from her right breast, and spat them out. Right away she was breathing again and recovered, but the young king had seen everything and did not know why Faithful Johannes had done it, and he grew furious about all this and shouted: "Throw him into prison!"

kniete und sog die drei Blutstropfen aus ihrer rechten Brust und speite sie aus. Alsbald athmete sie wieder und erholte sich, aber der junge König hatte es mit angesehen, und wußte nicht warum es der getreue Johannes gethan hatte, ward zornig darüber, und rief 'werft ihn ins Gefängnis.' Am andern Morgen ward der getreue Johannes verurtheilt und zum Galgen geführt, und als er oben stand und gerichtet werden sollte, sprach er 'jeder der sterben soll, darf vor seinem Ende noch einmal reden, soll ich das Recht auch haben?' 'Ja,' antwortete der König, 'es soll dir vergönnt sein.' Da sprach der treue Johannes 'Ich bin mit Unrecht verurtheilt und bin dir immer treu gewesen,' und erzählte wie er auf dem Meer das Gespräch der Raben gehört, und wie er, um seinen Herrn zu retten, das alles hätte thun müssen. Da rief der König 'o mein treuester Johannes, Gnade! Gnade! führt ihn herunter.' Aber der treue Johannes war bei dem letzten Wort das er geredet hatte leblos herabgefallen, und war ein Stein.

Darüber trug nun der König und die Königin großes Leid, und der König sprach 'ach, was hab ich große Treue so übel belohnt!' und ließ das steinerne Bild aufheben und in seine Schlafkammer neben sein Bett stellen. So oft er es ansah, weinte er und sprach 'ach, könnt ich dich wieder lebendig machen, mein getreuester Johannes.' Es gieng eine Zeit herum, da gebar die Königin Zwillinge, zwei Söhnlein, die wuchsen heran und waren ihre Freude. Einmal, als die Königin in der Kirche war, und die zwei Kinder bei dem Vater saßen und spielten, sah dieser wieder das steinerne Bildnis voll Trauer an, seufzte und rief 'ach, könnt ich dich wieder lebendig machen, mein getreuester Johannes.' Da fieng der Stein an zu reden und sprach 'ja, du kannst mich wieder lebendig machen, wenn du dein Liebstes daran wenden willst.' Da rief der König 'alles, was ich auf der Welt habe, will ich für dich hingeben.' Sprach der Stein weiter 'wenn du mit deiner eigenen Hand deinen beiden Kindern den Kopf abhaust und mich mit ihrem Blute bestreichst, so erhalte ich das Leben wieder.' Der König erschrak, als er hörte daß er seine liebsten Kinder selbst tödten sollte, doch dachte er an die große Treue, und daß der getreue Johannes für ihn gestorben war, zog sein Schwert und hieb mit eigener Hand den Kindern den Kopf ab. Und als er mit ihrem Blute den Stein bestrichen hatte, so kehrte das Leben zurück, und der getreue Johannes stand wieder frisch und gesund vor ihm. Er sprach zum König 'deine Treue soll nicht unbelohnt bleiben,' und nahm die Häupter der Kinder, setzte sie auf, und bestrich die Wunde mit ihrem Blut, davon

Next morning Faithful Johannes was sentenced and led to the gallows, and when he stood up there and was to be executed, he said: "Everyone who is to die may speak once more before his end. May I claim that right, too?" "Yes," replied the king, "it shall be granted to you." Then Faithful Johannes said: "I have been sentenced unjustly, and have always been faithful to you," and he recounted how, at sea, he had heard the conversation of the ravens, and how, in order to save his master, he had been obliged to do all that. At that the king exclaimed: "Oh, my most faithful Johannes, pardon! Pardon! Bring him down." But at the last word Faithful Johannes had uttered, he had fallen down lifeless, turned into stone.

Thereupon the king and the queen were suffering great pain, and the king said: "Ah, how very badly have I rewarded great faithfulness!" And he ordered the stone likeness to be lifted up and placed in his bedroom next to his bed. Whenever he looked at it, he wept and said: "Ah, if only I could bring you back to life, my most faithful Johannes." Some time passed; then the queen gave birth to twins, two little sons: they grew up and were her joy. Once, when the queen was at church and the two children were sitting beside their father and playing, he, full of grief, again looked at the stone likeness, sighed, and exclaimed: "Ah, if only I could bring you back again to life, my most faithful Johannes." Then the stone began to speak and said: "Yes, you can bring me back again to life, if you are willing to relinquish what you love most." At that the king exclaimed: "All I have in the world I want to sacrifice for you." The stone continued: "If you, with your own hand, cut off the heads of both of your children and cover me with their blood, I will be returned to life." The king was frightened when he heard that he himself was to kill his most beloved children, but he thought of that great faithfulness and of the death Faithful Johannes had suffered for him, drew his sword, and with his own hand cut off his children's heads. And when he had covered the stone with their blood, life came back to it, and once again Faithful Johannes stood before him, alive and well. He said to the king: "Your faithfulness shall not go unrewarded," and took the children's heads, put them back on, and covered the wounds with their blood: thus they were restored in a flash, jumped about and continued playing as if nothing had happened to them. Now the king was full of joy, and when he saw the queen coming, he hid Faithful Johannes and both of the children in a large cupboard. When she entered, he said to her: "Did you pray in church?" "Yes," she replied, "but I constantly thought of Faithful Johannes and of the great misfortune that befell him

wurden sie im Augenblick wieder heil, sprangen herum und spielten fort, als wär ihnen nichts geschehen. Nun war der König voll Freude, und als er die Königin kommen sah, versteckte er den getreuen Johannes und die beiden Kinder in einen großen Schrank. Wie sie hereintrat, sprach er zu ihr 'hast du gebetet in der Kirche?' 'Ja,' antwortete sie, 'aber ich habe beständig an den treuen Johannes gedacht, daß er so unglücklich durch uns geworden ist.' Da sprach er 'liebe Frau, wir können ihm das Leben wieder geben, aber es kostet uns unsere beiden Söhnlein, die müssen wir opfern.' Die Königin ward bleich und erschrak im Herzen, doch sprach sie 'wir sinds ihm schuldig wegen seiner großen Treue.' Da freute er sich daß sie dachte wie er gedacht hatte, gieng hin und schloß den Schrank auf, holte die Kinder und den treuen Johannes heraus und sprach 'Gott sei gelobt, er ist erlöst, und unsere Söhnlein haben wir auch wieder,' und erzählte ihr wie sich alles zugetragen hatte. Da lebten sie zusammen in Glückseligkeit bis an ihr Ende.[37]

because of us." Thereupon he said: *"Dear wife, we can give him back his life, but it will cost us our little sons: we will have to sacrifice them."* The queen turned pale, and was frightened at heart, but she said: *"We owe it to him because of his great faithfulness."* Then the king was happy that she thought as he had thought; and he went and opened the cupboard, brought out the children and Faithful Johannes, and said: *"God be praised, he is saved, and moreover we have our little sons again,"* and he told her how everything had happened. Then they lived together blissfully to the end of their days.

8

The Idiom of Passion: "Faithful Johannes"

> Walk with me. Hand in hand through the nightmare of narrative, the neat sentences secret-nailed over meaning.
>
> JEANETTE WINTERSON
> *Gut Symmetries*

A narrative of early desire and of discordances resolved at the price of familial slaughter, "Faithful Johannes" perpetuates the lie of its tale in the eventual happiness of its conjugal couple. Visions of oneness drive and split a narrative thread that all but connects at times with an absent mother and a world of bloody and blissful experience. At other times, in the progressions of the dominant plot, resolutions appear in self-assured, fairy-tale jubilance. Yet the very notion of selfhood fractures time and again in the story that underlies "Faithful Johannes." Johannes himself aims at an impossible convergence of past, present, and future: able to hear and willing to adhere to both early preverbal and linguistically set communications, he risks and loses his human embodiment. The plot, which will not let him stand as a stone statue in the king's bedroom forever, generates happy words at its end. The story meanwhile waits in the wings. Everpresent, and never articulated in a language of conceptual differentiation, it reverberates in ambivalent formulations, surfaces in unspeakable sights, and resounds in avian conversations. You hear this story once you forgo your need to know. It is a story before and beyond certitude as well as ossification. Bones are cut and put together again; a body turns to stone and suddenly to flesh again; blood is sucked from a forbidden breast: such a story will not end on time.

Between Affect and Articulation

The promise the dying king elicits from his favorite servant, Johannes, seems straightforward enough. He wants him to be his son's foster father and to teach him everything he should know. To this Johannes replies that he will never desert the son, and will serve him faithfully. The king now specifies that Johannes show his son the entire castle after his death, except for the last chamber on the long corridor. If his son were to see the portrait of the Princess of the Golden Roof hidden in this chamber, the king states, he would fall in love with the likeness and be exposed to great perils for her sake. Johannes renews his promise, *Versprechen*, whereupon the king falls silent and dies.

Once again, the word for promise, *Versprechen*, is fraught with an ambivalence in which the linguistic tensions between "promise" and "erroneous utterance" play out forcefully.[38] Johannes will uphold his faithfulness under the sway of a promise turned nightmare.

Versprechen in "Faithful Johannes" is doubly associated with seeing and its cessation at the time of death. Were the promise not given, it would commit the king to a reluctant departure, his eyes straining to remain open, breaking into a final blank stare. Once Johannes has given the promise, the king adds a specification regarding the hidden portrait: he will close his eyes on the condition that his son will not be allowed to open his own to a painting whose allure would subject him to great danger.

In his faithfulness, Johannes embodies the whole range of *Versprechen*. He both keeps and breaks his promise to the old king, by extending its range beyond the specific wish the king had attached to it. Remaining within the scope of *Versprechen*, he nevertheless oversteps the boundary drawn by the king. Johannes' faithfulness derives from the multivalent core of his promise. In his *Versprechen* and its interrelationship with error, the father's past and the son's future touch upon each other with calamitous consequences.

As taken on by Johannes, the promise separates father and son in a manner that brings the old king into the proximity of Bluebeard. As in the Bluebeard tale, there is a forbidden chamber not to be entered. In both situations, the castle around this chamber is lavishly furnished and filled with riches. When the door opens, in either tale, a shock jolts the one who enters into the room.[39]

The parallels seem to end here, for while Bluebeard's chamber contains corpses and blood, the chamber that awaits the son holds the most beautiful portrait. Clearly, the son and successor does not share the fate of the wife who steps into Bluebeard's secret room. A less obvious story, however, has begun to unfold.

There is no queen in "Faithful Johannes." Not even the death of one is mentioned. Yet the painting exudes the intensity of very early memories, "such as aesthetic experience when a person feels uncannily embraced by an object."[40] When the son sees the portrait for the first time, it is as if he knows, and feels, everything about the figure. The tale has announced this moment as the one at which he will fall unconscious, become "ohnmächtig" (74), "without power." Just before this happens he is standing on his tiptoes, looking over the servant's shoulder, seeming more like a little boy than the king he is said to be. Having lost his consciousness, he is put onto his bed, "until he was himself again" (75).

The freshly aware king, speaking his "first words" (75), passionately embraces the *Schein* before him. The words that follow connect with a time of prelinguistic bliss. The portrait's beauty coalesces with a sense of communication before the onset of distinctly differentiated speech: "My love for her is so great that if all the leaves on the trees were tongues they could not express it..." (75). In a further departure from bounded spheres, the word "Blätter" (74), "leaves," conjures up both vegetative life and books.

The king's first words are charged with the emotional intensity of his enraptured collapse: "Ah, who is that beautiful likeness?" (75).[41] This exclamation captures the lover's experience in its *Schein* between reality and a sight before consciousness. Like the protagonists in "The Glass Coffin"—the tailor at the hut's threshold, and the young woman in her bedroom—he is gripped by an experience in a space before clear-cut distinctions between individual identity and its aesthetic representation. At this moment, the painting itself is the focus of desire.

In due time, events and experiences before verbal expression will defy words. As the narrative unfolds in its uncanny closeness to the mother figure whom the young protagonist only knows from a time before words, it is propelled into infanticidal violence. At this initial point, the king asserts: "I will risk my life to win her," putting his servant's life at risk as well: "You are my most faithful Johannes, you must help me" (75).

The journey toward the living embodiment of the likeness before the king stays close to home, although in terms of the plot his ship crosses the sea. Once in the desired land, Johannes sees a beautiful maiden in the castle's courtyard, drawing water from the well. About to carry the "glistening" (77) fluid away in her golden buckets, she turns around and sees the stranger. Did Johannes' shadow fall onto the water's shiny, pulsating surface? The contact between the Princess of the Golden Roof and the king begins to take shape in correspondence with the portrait that "glittered" (75) in its golden splendor. In making room for the stranger's shadow, the narrative evokes a first encounter that has not yet acquired more definite contours. Delicately responsive mirrorings occur here in an emergent visual field in which, as with *Versprechen*, linguistic articulation barely, if at all, is commencing to take hold.

As the tale moves toward a recognition of more defined figures, objects of exchange and trickery come to the fore. Guided by Johannes, the king now poses as a merchant. On his way toward a decidedly objective realm, this commercial figure is intent on converting the portrait's *Schein* into a reality he can take home on his ship. For him, riches and seafaring are connected with each other, as at the beginning of "The King of the Golden Mountain." Yet unlike the merchant who stays ashore as his ships are sent on their missions, the new king is about to travel with his wares on the waters. Less objectively distanced than the paternal figure in the mountain tale, he is nevertheless on his way toward the realm of things, and of the beguiling figure whose image he has, thus far, only seen in the framework of his original home.

As the princess and the king are about to meet in terms of exchange, prelinguistic forces about to be left behind reassert themselves. "Faithful Johannes" continues to illuminate intricacies of an all-encompassing process, and speaks of moments that are both decisive and marginal. The portrait, turned reality in the space of fiction, prefigures the early world of *Schein* in the words that lure the princess onto the ship. In announcing "the most artful and delightful things ever made of gold" (77), Johannes adds further resonance to glittering, fluid occurrences: most delightful, "köstlichste" (76), objects bring up "Kost," "nourishment," oral pleasures along with the allure of "most artful" creations.

As the princess connects with the treasures through "curiosity and desire" (77), she revives the portrait from which she is meant to emerge as a consequence of the king's journey. Through his wares of exchange, the king has unwittingly recreated the scene before her likeness. Her intense interest and "desire," "Lust" (76), which connotes "lust," recall his powerful affect. The princess desires to "view your master's treasures" (77). Viewing, in the framework of early wishfulness, and the activities of a more objective world go hand in hand here. The treasures stimulate the wish to own them, and they also stir the desire to indulge in the pleasures of appearance. At any moment in this constellation, *Schein* may return with the portrait intact, as if the king had never boarded his ship. The narrative's atmosphere in its complex reverberations, then, does not reflect the developmental lines produced by the plot.

Resisting interpretive closure, such narratives tell stories apart from storylines. Linguistic multivalence, repetitions and variations of images, as well as obscure echoes of earlier occurrences signal something else than a fairy tale in its progressive unfolding. In its neglect of the underlying story, the overt tale functions as a cover-up.

Violence and abuse underneath and before surface events tend to be disconnected from fairy-tale plots. Discussions of cruelties that do not take note of these more deeply seated torments run the risk of reenforcing such disconnections.

There is a preset congruence between surface events and a procedure that explores their symbolic depth dimension within a linguistic framework. In both domains, language reigns in its semantically evolved forms. The more explicit the uncovering of the depth dimension, the more buried underneath the words is the realm before linguistic articulation.

In this realm, something happened once before a time. Something before plots and words presents itself, away from the tales, in stories waiting to be seen and felt. Listening for these stories does not imply an abolition of significance throughout. Time and again, fairy-story experience involves a return of memory. A countertransferential understanding sets in that can be experienced, but hardly yet cast into words.[42] A feeling, an atmosphere from long ago registers, but does not enter into a linguistically stable state.

Avian Speech: Recollective Intimations

Once on the ship, the princess is more fully drawn into the underlying story. Having spent hours looking at the golden treasures, much like the king once did in exploring his castle after his father's death, she suddenly realizes that the ship has set sail and that she is a captive. The king, however, manages to display himself as trustworthy and explains his royal, rather than merely mercantile, status. It seems the tale has arrived in a relatively objective terrain, away from the portrait's *Schein*.

However, the king's concomitant reference to his first viewing of the portrait, when he "fell to the ground in a faint" (75), creates a renewed sense of uncertainty: does he view the princess as a portrait after all? On the "high seas" (79), such uncertainty develops more strongly. Reminiscent of the events surrounding the stranger's music in "The Glass Coffin," delimitations turn permeable in the wake of the music Johannes plays. Animals who appeared to be mere things to be traded and admired now break out of their isolation and speak. Through his ability to understand the ravens' conversation above the ship, Johannes links the narrative with its earlier time. When the king had awoken from his unconsciousness in front of the portrait, he had envisioned tongues on the trees. Now nature speaks again.

In their temporal awareness, the three birds transcend and precede the chronologically defined time in which the king and the princess are sailing across the sea: what happened in the context of the portrait has not come to an end. The narrative connects the birds with a past about to be revived.[43] "Set all sails to make it fly like a bird in the air" (77), Johannes had ordered the ship's crew at the beginning of the journey back to the kingdom. The ship in the air highlights the experience of an imagination unbound. Once again, Johannes brings to life the far reach of *Versprechen*. He had been able to speak to the dying king and to the son in a borderline range of seeing and of an intensely experiential multivalence. On the ship, he "caught sight" (79) of the ravens and heard their talk of the past and the future.

Language is explicitly redefined here as including the communication between the birds. The ravens speak in a language that recalls the immediacy of early utterances. The king has just remembered the "first" (79) time he saw the portrait. Distinctly audible in the act of storytelling, a *da* rhythm develops: "da" occurs again and again, reminiscent of first steps into verbalization as well as of a language before and beyond lexical specificity. "Da" happens to occur inconspicuously, so much so that it is easily dropped in translation. In such instances, which frequently take place in Grimms' fairy tales—such as "The King of the Golden Mountain"—nothing seems to be at stake. "Da," it then appears, is a mere expletive, something the sentence and the narrative can do without. The "da" that turns invisible on the way from one language to another, however, marks a spot before and beyond preset comprehension, and indicates the incipient versatility of the nascent as well as vibrantly superfluous word.

Early forms of children's single word speech come to mind here: distinctly contoured utterances that resist translation into a particular vocabulary, traversing a multitude of dictionaries with ease and instant relevance. "Dada," Hugo Ball asserts in a related context, is an "international word," and: "I want the word where it ends and where it begins. Dada is the heart of the words."[44]

The ravens' speech abounds with childhood themes. It might be tempting to relate the red horse the king—according to the first raven—will wish to mount to an advanced phase in his development. In this vein, the image of the king soaring up into the air never to be seen again by his lady might imply a rebellious sexuality in the face of an impending marriage. The underlying narrative, however, suggests otherwise. The passion that will grip the king recalls his response at the first sight of the portrait. His love, it seems, is about to reappear in its original intensity. Upon returning home, he will be tempted to return to the princess he knew before he met her in person. In the context of the underlying story, this temptation is further fed by the memory of the mother before words.

Even the first moment at which the king sees the princess outside of the picture invokes both stories, the one in which he is intensely affected by her, and the one in which he focuses on her foreground appearance. The comparison whereby the king relates the latter figure favorably to the portrait, perceiving that "her beauty was even greater than represented"—"dargestellt" (76)—"in the likeness," somewhat suppresses the earlier encounter, which explicitly transcends representational language. The linguistic statement hardly meshes with the shock of beauty, a divergence rendered invisible in Manheim's streamlined translation in which the king saw "that she was even more beautiful than her portrait" (25).

As the ship sails on, the second raven predicts a fire that will burn its way through clothing and skin to the "marrow" (79) of the king's bones. In this vision, nothing remains of the nuptial robe of gold and silver, for it actually consists of sulfur and pitch. The story of passion and the skeletons in its range reappear with a force that melts down the distinctions of daytime reality. It is not the bride but the king who will wish to wear the "bridal robe" (79).

Reminiscent of the weddings in "The King of the Golden Mountain" and "The Glass Coffin," the story underneath the plot of "Faithful Johannes" tells of a wedding on the verge of a deeply felt discordance. The third raven's prediction creates a contrast to the hot, red colors that characterize the king's anticipated passion. The queen, whose heart has opened up to him in a less ardent manner to begin with, now is at risk of turning "pale" (81) in sudden collapse. If she is to survive, still more redness needs to be extracted from her. In an act best performed by a vampire, Johannes will suck three drops of blood from her right breast and spit them out.

The king's passion and the queen's paleness expose their wedding as a foreground event. The king moves more strongly into the universe he had encountered in the painting. In this context, the queen's breast is an organ of death and life recalling the unnamed mother at his origins. Life and death, beginning and end exist here in close, and harshly accentuated proximity.

The vicissitudes of *Versprechen*, in which life and death intertwine, reappear in the immediate environment of the life-saving intervention. If someone reveals, "verräth" (80), the requirements of the rescue, "his entire body would be turned to stone, from the top of his spine to his toes" (81). The dissolution—*Verrat*—of a promise coalesces with the matter of life and death that informs the underlying story from its very beginning. Again, the narrative's linguistic embodiment speaks. In an oddly suggestive formulation, the spine's top appears as "Wirbel" (80), which includes "whirl," "maelstrom," in its semantic range. The stone into which the protagonist of *Versprechen* will turn materializes in the course of a rapid descent.

Johannes makes his own contribution to this trajectory. He carries out the first two tasks as suggested by the ravens, but he changes the envisioned procedure for the queen's rescue. The third raven had spoken of lifting the unconscious queen in preparation for the sucking and spitting. Johannes, however, introduces elements of the *Versprechen* into the narrative. He lifts her up, but rather than immediately proceeding to extract the blood from her breast—she is on the verge of dying—he carries her into a "chamber" (81). The royal figure now is in a room like the one that housed her portrait. Her first dancing steps following the wedding ceremony have not led into a new life, but into the immediate proximity of the *Schein* in which she once existed. Johannes' *Versprechen* to the dying king, a matter of life and death for the royal son, comes alive again as the bride is close to death.

In his departure from the rescue procedure, Johannes takes more time than allotted to him in the ravens' conversation. Time itself transforms in this elaboration. Increasingly Johannes demonstrates his faithfulness to a story of repetition in which the original, multivalent *Versprechen* and the experience of *Schein* in front of the portrait reoccur with striking precision. In the chamber of the present and the past, Johannes lays down the queen. He reenacts the scene before the portrait. Just as he lifted the unconscious king from the ground, carried him off, and laid him down, so he now does with the queen.

Acting in the multidimensional terrain of *Versprechen* as both the old king's faithful servant and the new one's foster parent, Johannes enables the tale to move forward on the level of the plot, and simultaneously to revive the intensities of a preobjective, passionate past. Yet as the narrative's tensions continue to coalesce in Johannes, he finally enters into the realm of death.

Through Johannes, the tale had eluded its lie: that life in its splendor could unfold outside of the chamber's compelling sphere. Now the narrative is approaching its impasse. Johannes is thrown into prison, judged to be guilty, and taken to the gallows. From the king's perspective, the servant's breast-sucking has only been the latest and most severe in a series of transgressions. Johannes, he perceives, has shot the red horse and destroyed the bridal garment. Now the king's patience is at its end. The narrative's tensions are about to erupt.

At the gallows, Johannes tells the king of the avian conversation, thereby committing, as the ravens had anticipated, an act of treason, *Verrat*. Secret knowledge, which is closely connected with the hidden narrative, now appears in the tale for all to see. No longer will the royal couple be able to carry on its foreground life. Without Johannes, the conduit between past and present, the tale to come will be starkly explicit.

Forced Conclusions

Johannes turns into a stone statue, "steinerne Bild" (82), whose semantic spectrum includes "stone image" and "stone painting." The "Bild" (72), "likeness," of the Princess of the Golden Roof cross-connects with his ossified state. For some time, however, the plot goes on while the stone statue sits by the bed, its living precursor not forgotten, but apparently not needed for the family to unfold. Twins are born, two little boys who become the queen's "joy" (83). The father hardly appears to share in this delight. The tale presents him as attached to the stony likeness, "steinerne Bildnis" (82), even when his children are with him, playing while their mother is at church. With this father figure but dimly aware of his present life, the stage is set for sudden change.

Having been dormant for years, the underlying narrative reenters the tale. The figure from the king's distant past begins to speak: Johannes can come back to life if the king is willing to sacrifice, "daran wenden" (82), what he loves most. In addition to "relinquishment" and "sacrifice," "daran wenden" resonates with "investment" and "turn," "Wende." Love, investment, and a potential turn form a tight knot about to unravel. Feeling and a commercially tinged activity combine closely at the onset of a cataclysmic event.

"If you, with your own hand," the voice announces, "cut off the heads of both of your children and cover me with their blood, I will be returned to life" (83). Hearing this, the father is not "horrified," as has been suggested (Manheim 28); he is "frightened," "erschrack" (82). In the face of the unthinkable, he retains some equilibrium: he "thought" (83) of Johannes' faithfulness and sacrifice for him. As the king rapidly—in the course of a single sentence—moves from being scared to thinking, he acts as if in shock. He does not appear to feel the full impact of the proposal: a presence of the past asserts itself.

Through his voice out of the stone, Johannes is there to be experienced, but this time he remains absent as the mediator between the king's pursuit of an ambitious adulthood and the world of *Versprechen* and *Schein*. Early, intense feelings return in the voice of the servant and foster father, but no firm place is provided for them in the king's current life. The stone that speaks does revive the king's vitality; at the same time, however, his ties to his children all but dissolve. Past and present do not clash here; the latter is overwhelmed by the former in the moment of a sentence.

The sentence that begins with the scare and continues with thoughts of faithfulness ends precipitously: the father acts immediately, draws his sword, and cuts off his children's heads. Hardly any time passes before Johannes stands before him, "alive and well" (83). Life itself seems to have returned: "the," "das" (82), life comes back, the text says of Johannes' reappearance.

In the company of Johannes, the king finds himself in the realm of the father, the portrait, and of the elusive mother figure. His own fatherhood, in which he seemed to have departed from his early involvements, has vanished from the scene. If the decapitation of the children evokes the shadow queen in the Bluebeardian chamber from the beginning of "Faithful Johannes," the narrative touches upon maternal origins.[45]

As does the protagonist of "The King of the Golden Mountain," the husband and son in "Faithful Johannes" returns to the sphere of his parents, with the wife's feelings all but ignored. The queen's "joy" (83) has been destroyed. In "The King of the Golden Mountain," the queen's explicit wish not to be brought to her husband's father had been disregarded. In both tales the same kind of violence erupts; heads are cut off, and the sword of the Golden Mountain quite possibly extends its deadly work to the protagonist's familial territory as well. Echoes of an earlier time also pervade "The Glass Coffin": the shots fired by the female protagonist tell of a deeply rooted anger similar to the fury of the head-cutting King of the Golden Mountain.

The son-turned-king in "Faithful Johannes" does not exhibit such signs of anger, nor does he seem to show the marks of abuse suffered by the son of the rich merchant and the daughter of the rich duke. Yet the murder of his twin sons resonates with the story of the mountain king's life. Does the king in "Faithful Johannes," furthermore, bear the mark of a murdered mother? If the locked chamber with the portrait recalls Bluebeard's secret, the *Versprechen* the dying king extracts from Johannes also involves a *Schein* whose force is connected with the never-mentioned mother figure. Although not directly maternal, blood in "Faithful Johannes" gives pause for still further regard: sucked from the queen's breast, spurting from the children's necks, rubbed onto stony Johannes, the red fluid shares its color with the horse of boundless passion. The new king of "Faithful Johannes" traverses the terrain of the furious little boy in "The King of the Golden Mountain," and of the maiden who fires the shot in "The Glass Coffin."

"Faithful Johannes," to be sure, celebrates a happy ending. Restored to life, the twins play on "as if nothing had happened to them. Now the king was full of joy..." (83). His children reflect his own disconnections. Despite having just had their heads cut off, they behave as if their lives were unfolding blissfully. They, the king, and Johannes perform a trick so that their tale can come to a close. With Johannes and the twins hidden in a cupboard, the queen is put to the test. Would she cut off her children's heads in order to revive Johannes? The king uses the palatable word "sacrifice" (85) to put the question to his wife. After a brief hesitation, she replies to her happy husband in the affirmative. Finally beyond the guilt and the memory that had haunted their lives in the wake of the *Versprechen*, the royal family has reached the flat surface of the plot: "Then they lived together blissfully to the end of their days" (85).

9

Brüder Grimm
Von dem Machandelboom[46]

Dat is nu all lang heer, wol twe dusend Johr, do wöör dar en ryk Mann, de hadd ene schöne frame Fru, un se hadden sik beyde sehr leef, hadden awerst kene Kinner, se wünschden sik awerst sehr welke, un de Fru bedd'd so veel dorüm Dag un Nacht, man se kregen keen un kregen keen. Vör erem Huse wöör en Hof, dorup stünn en Machandelboom, ünner dem stünn de Fru eens im Winter un schelld sik enen Appel, un as se sik den Appel so schelld, so sneet se sik in'n Finger un dat Blood feel in den Snee. 'Ach,' säd de Fru, un süft'd so recht hoog up, un seg dat Blood vör sik an, un wöör so recht wehmödig, 'hadd ik doch en Kind, so rood as Blood un so witt as Snee.' Un as se dat säd, so wurr ehr so recht fröhlich to Mode: ehr wöör recht, as schull dat wat warden. Do güng se to dem Huse, un't güng een Maand hen, de Snee vorgüng: un twe Maand, do wöör dat gröön: un dre Maand, do kömen de Blömer uut der Eerd: un veer Maand, do drungen sik alle Bömer in dat Holt, un de grönen Twyge wören all in eenanner wussen: door süngen de Vögelkens dat dat ganße Holt schalld, un de Blöiten felen von den Bömern: do wöör de fofte Maand wech, un se stünn ünner dem Machandelboom, de röök so schön, do sprüng ehr dat Hart vör Freuden, un se füll up ere Knee un kunn sik nich laten: un as de soste Maand vorby wöör, do wurren de Früchte dick un staark, do wurr se ganß still: un de söwde Maand, do greep se na den Machandelbeeren un eet se so nydsch, do wurr se trurig un krank: do güng de achte Maand hen, un se reep eren Mann un weend un säd 'wenn ik staarw, so begraaf my ünner den Machandelboom.' Do wurr se ganß getrost, un freude sik, bet de neegte Maand vorby wöör, do kreeg se en Kind so witt as Snee un so rood as Blood, un as se dat seeg, so freude se sik so, dat se stürw.

Do begroof ehr Mann se ünner den Machandelboom, un he füng an to wenen so sehr: ene Tyd lang, do wurr dat wat sachter, un do he noch wat weend hadd, do hüll he up, un noch en Tyd, do nöhm he sik wedder ene Fru.

The Juniper Tree

*A*ll this happened a long time ago, probably two thousand years ago. In those days there was a rich man who had a beautiful and pious wife, and they loved each other very much. They had, however, no children; but they very much wished for them, and the woman prayed so much for them day and night: still they had none. In front of their house, there was a yard, and in it stood a juniper tree, under which the woman once stood in the winter and peeled herself an apple, and as she was peeling the apple she cut her finger, and her blood fell on the snow. "Ah," said the woman with a deep sigh, and looked at the blood before her, and grew very sad, "if only I had a child as red as blood and as white as snow." And when she had said that, she grew very happy: she very much felt that something would come of it. Then she went to her house, and a month passed by, and the snow disappeared; two months, and now everything was green; three months, and now the flowers came out of the ground; four months, and now all the trees grew wider, and all the green branches were intertwined; now the little birds sang so that the whole forest resounded, and the blossoms fell from the trees; and now the fifth month had passed, and she stood under the juniper tree: it smelled so beautifully, and now her heart leapt for joy, and she fell down on her knees and was beside herself with jubilation; and when the sixth month had passed, the fruits were big and firm, and now she became very still; and in the seventh month she snatched at the juniper berries and ate them most greedily, and now she became sad and sick; then the eighth month passed by, and she called her husband, and wept and said: "If I die, bury me under the juniper tree." Now she felt quite consoled, and she was happy until the next month had passed; then she had a child as white as snow and as red as blood, and when she saw it, she was so happy that she died.

Then her husband buried her under the juniper tree, and he began to weep a lot; after a while, that diminished a bit, and when he had wept a bit

Mit de tweden Fru kreeg he ene Dochter, dat Kind awerst von der eersten Fru wöör en lüttje Sähn, un wöör so rood as Blood un so witt as Snee. Wenn de Fru ere Dochter so anseeg, so hadd se se so leef, awerst denn seeg se den lüttjen Jung an, un dat güng ehr so dorch't Hart, un ehr düchd as stünn he ehr allerwegen im Weg, un dachd denn man jümmer wo se ehr Dochter all das Vörmägent towenden wull, un de Böse gaf ehr dat in, dat se dem lüttjen Jung ganß gramm wurr un stödd em herüm von een Eck in de anner, un buffd em hier un knuffd em door, so dat dat aarme Kind jümmer in Angst wöör. Wenn he denn uut de School köhm, so hadd he kene ruhige Städ.

Eens wöör de Fru up de Kamer gaan, do köhm de lüttje Dochter ook herup un säd 'Moder, gif my enen Appel.' 'Ja, myn Kind' säd de Fru un gaf ehr enen schönen Appel uut der Kist; de Kist awerst hadd enen grooten sworen Deckel mit en groot schaarp ysern Slott. 'Moder,' säd de lüttje Dochter, 'schall Broder nich ook enen hebben?' Dat vördrööt de Fru, doch säd se 'ja, wenn he uut de School kummt.' Un as se uut dat Fenster wohr wurr dat he köhm, so wöör dat recht, as wenn de Böse äwer ehr köhm, un se grappst to un nöhm erer Dochter den Appel wedder wech un säd 'du schalst nich ehr enen hebben as Broder.' Do smeet se den Appel in de Kist un maakd de Kist to: do köhm de lüttje Jung in de Döhr, do gaf ehr de Böse in dat se fründlich to em säd 'myn Sähn, wullt du enen Appel hebben?' un seeg em so hastig an. 'Moder,' säd de lüttje Jung, 'wat sühst du gräsig uut! ja, gif my enen Appel.' Do wöör ehr as schull se em toreden. 'Kumm mit my,' säd se un maakd den Deckel up, 'hahl dy enen Appel heruut.' Un as sik de lüttje Jung henin bückd, so reet ehr de Böse, bratsch! slöög se den Deckel to dat de Kopp afflöög un ünner de roden Appel füll. Da äwerleep ehr dat in de Angst, un dachd 'kunn ik dat von my bringen!' Da güng se bawen na ere Stuw na erem Draagkasten un hahl' uut de bäwelste Schuuflad enen witten Dook, un sett't den Kopp wedder up den Hals un bünd den Halsdook so üm, dat'n niks sehn kunn, un sett't em vör de Döhr up enen Stohl un gaf em den Appel in de Hand.

Do köhm doorna Marleenken to erer Moder in de Kääk de stünn by dem Führ un hadd enen Putt mit heet Water vör sik, den röhrd se jümmer üm. 'Moder,' säd Marleenken, 'Broder sitt vör de Döhr un süht ganß witt uut un hett enen Appel in de Hand, ik heb em beden he schull my den Appel gewen, awerst he antwöörd my nich, do wurr my ganß grolich.' 'Gah nochmaal hen,' säd de Moder, 'un wenn he dy nich antworden will, so gif em eens an de more, he stopped; and after another while he took a new wife.

With this second wife he had a daughter; but the first wife's child was a little son, and he was as red as blood and as white as snow. When the woman looked at her daughter, she loved her so much; but then she looked at the little boy, and that made her feel sick at heart, and it seemed to her as if he always stood in her way, and she kept thinking about how she could get the whole fortune for her daughter; and the Evil One imbued her with this, so that she was very upset at the little boy, and she pushed him around from one corner to the other, and hit him here and poked him there, so that the poor child always lived in fear. So when he came from school, there was no quiet place for him.

Once the woman had gone up to her chamber, and her little daughter went up, too, and said: "Mother, give me an apple." "Yes, my child," said the woman and gave her a beautiful apple from the chest; but the chest had a large heavy lid with a large sharp iron lock. "Mother," said the little daughter, "shall my brother not have one, too?" That annoyed the woman, but she said: "Yes, when he comes home from school." And when she saw from the window that he was coming, it was just as if the Evil One overcame her, and she snatched at the apple and took it away from her daughter, and said: "You shall not have one before your brother." Then she threw the apple into the chest and shut it; then the little boy came through the door, and then the Evil One made her say to him in a friendly manner: "My son, do you want to have an apple?" and she looked at him full of wickedness. "Mother," said the little boy, "how grisly you look! Yes, give me an apple." Now she felt as if she should encourage him. "Come with me," she said and raised the lid, "take out an apple." And as the little boy bent into the chest, the Evil One swayed her, and crunch! she slammed the lid shut so that his head flew off and fell among the red apples. Then she was overcome with fear and thought: "If only I could get rid of this problem!" Then she went up to her room to her chest of drawers, and took a white cloth from the top drawer, and set the head back on the neck and wrapped the cloth around it so that nothing could be seen, and set him on a chair in front of the door, and placed the apple in his hand.

After a while Marleenken came into the kitchen to her mother, who was standing by the fire in front of a pot of hot water, which she kept stirring. "Mother," said Marleenken, "brother is sitting in front of the door and looks very white and has an apple in his hand. I asked him to give me the apple, but he did not answer me, and I felt terribly frightened." "Go there again," said

Oren.' Do güng Marleenken hen un säd, 'Broder, gif my den Appel.' Awerst he sweeg still, do gaf se em eens up de Oren, do feel de Kopp herünn, doräwer vörschrock se sik un füng an to wenen un to roren, un löp to erer Moder un säd 'ach, Moder, ik hebb mynem Broder den Kopp afslagen,' un weend un weend un wull sik nich tofreden gewen. 'Marleenken,' säd de Moder, 'wat hest du dahn! awerst swyg man still, dat et keen Mensch maarkt, dat is nu doch nich to ännern; wy willen em in Suhr kaken.' Do nöhm de Moder den lüttjen Jung un hackd em in Stücken, ded de in den Putt un kaakd em in Suhr. Marleenken awerst stünn daarby un weend un weend, un de Tranen füllen all in den Putt un se bruukden goor keen Solt.

Da köhm de Vader to Huus un sett't sik to Disch un säd 'wo is denn myn Sähn?' Da droog de Moder ene groote groote Schöttel up mit Swartsuhr, un Marleeken weend un kunn sich nich hollen. Do säd de Vader wedder 'wo is denn myn Sähn?' 'Ach,' säd de Moder, 'he is äwer Land gaan, na Mütten erer Grootöhm: he wull door wat blywen.' 'Wat dait he denn door? un heft my nich maal Adjüüs sechd!' 'O he wull geern hen un bed my of he door wol sos Wäken blywen kunn; he is jo woll door uphawen.' 'Ach,' säd de Mann, 'my is so recht trurig dat is doch nicht recht, he hadd my doch Adjüüs sagen schullt.' Mit des füng he an to äten un säd 'Marleenken, wat weenst du? Broder wart wol wedder kamen.' 'Ach, Fru,' säd he do, 'wat smeckt my dat Äten schöön? gif my mehr!' Un je mehr he eet, je mehr wull he hebben, un säd 'geeft my mehr, gy schöhlt niks door af hebben, dat is as wenn dat all myn wör.' Un he eet un eet, un de Knakens smeet he all ünner den Disch, bet he allens up hadd. Marleenken awerst güng hen na ere Commod un nöhm ut de ünnerste Schuuf eren besten syden Dook, un hahl all de Beenkens un Knakens ünner den Disch heruut un bünd se in den syden Dook un droog se vör de Döhr un weend ere blödigen Tranen. Door läd se se ünner den Machandelboom in dat gröne Gras, un as se se door henlechd hadd', so war ehr mit eenmal so recht licht, un weend nich mer. Do füng de Machandelboom an sik to bewegen, un de Twyge deden sik jümmer so recht von eenanner, un denn wedder tohoop, so recht as wenn sik eener so recht freut un mit de Händ so dait. Mit des so güng dar so'n Newel von dem Boom un recht in dem Newel dar brennd dat as Führ, un uut dem Führ dar flöög so'n schönen Vagel heruut, de süng so herrlich und flöög hoog in de Luft, un as he wech wöör, do wöör de Machandelboom as he vörhen west wöör, un de Dook mit de Knakens wöör wech. Marleeken awerst wöör so recht licht un

the mother, "and if he does not want to answer you, give him a slap in the face." So Marleenken went there and said: "Brother, give me the apple." But he was silent, so she gave him a slap in the face, whereupon his head fell down, at which she was frightened and began to weep and to scream, and she ran to her mother and said: "Ah, mother, I have knocked my brother's head off," and she wept and wept and would not calm down. "Marleenken," said the mother, "what have you done! But be quiet, so that no one will notice, it cannot be helped now anyway; we will make him into a stew with blood sauce." Then the mother took the little boy and chopped him into pieces, put them into the pot, and made him into a stew with blood sauce. But Marleenken stood there and wept and wept, and all of her tears fell into the pot, and no salt at all was needed.

Then the father came home and sat down to table and said: "But where is my son?" Then the mother served a large, large dish of stew with blood sauce, and Marleenken wept and could not stop. Then the father said again: "But where is my son?" "Ah," said the mother, "he has gone across the country to his mother's great-uncle: he wants to stay there for awhile." "What is he doing there? And he did not even say good-bye to me!" "Oh, he really wanted to go and asked me if he might stay there for six weeks; after all he is well taken care of there." "Ah," said the man, "I feel so sad, that was not right: he should have said good-bye to me." With that he began to eat and said: "Marleenken, why are you weeping? Your brother will surely come back." "Ah, wife," he then said, "how good this meal tastes to me! Give me more!" And the more he ate the more he wanted, and he said: "Give me more, you shall have none of this, it feels as if all of it were mine." And he ate and ate, and he threw all the bones under the table, until he had eaten everything. But Marleenken went to her chest of drawers, and took her best silk cloth out of the bottom drawer, and got all the little bones from under the table, and tied them up in the silk cloth, and carried them outside the door, and cried bitterly. Then she lay down under the juniper tree on the green grass, and when she had lain down there, she suddenly felt quite lighthearted and cried no more. Now the juniper tree began to move, and its branches spread apart and came together again, just as when one is very happy and claps with one's hands. At the same time, a kind of fog rose from the tree, and in the midst of this fog it burned like fire, and out of the fire there flew a beautiful bird, singing so wonderfully, and he flew high into the air, and when he was *vörgnöögt, recht as wenn de Broder noch leewd. Do güng se wedder ganß lustig in dat Huus by Disch un eet.*

 De Vagel awerst flöög wech un sett't sik up enen Goldsmidt syn Huus un füng an to singen
   '*mein Mutter der mich schlacht,*
   mein Vater der mich aß,
   mein Schwester der Marlenichen
   sucht alle meine Benichen,
   bindt sie in ein seiden Tuch,
   legt's unter den Machandelbaum.
   Kywitt, kywitt, wat vör'n schöön Vagel bün ik!'

 De Goldsmidt seet in syn Waarkstäd un maakd ene gollne Kede, do höörd he den Vagel, de up syn Dack seet un süng, un dat dünkd em so schöön. Da stünn he up, un as he äwer den Süll güng, do vörlöör he eenen Tüffel. He güng awer so recht midden up de Strat hen, eenen Tüffel un een Sock an: syn Schortfell hadd he vör, un in de een Hand hadd he de golln Kede un in de anner de Tang; un de Sünn schynd so hell up de Strat. Door güng he recht so staan un seeg den Vagel an. 'Vagel,' secht he do, 'wo schöön kanst du singen! Sing my dat Stück nochmaal.' 'Ne,' secht de Vagel, 'twemaal sing ik nich umsünst. Gif my de golln Kede, so will ik dy't nochmaal singen.' 'Door,' secht de Goldsmidt, 'hest du de golln Kede, nu sing my dat nochmaal.' Do köhm de Vagel un nöhm de golln Kede so in de rechte Poot, un güng vor den goldsmidt sitten un süng
   '*mein Mutter der mich schlacht,*
   mein Vater der mich aß,
   mein Schwester der Marlenichen
   sucht alle meine Benichen,
   bindt sie in ein seiden Tuch,
   legts unter den Machandelbaum.
   Kywitt, kywitt, was vör'n schöön Vagel bün ik!'

 Do flög de Vagel wach na enem Schooster, un sett't sik up den syn Dack un süng
   '*mein Mutter der mich schlacht,*
   mein Vater der mich aß,
   mein Schwester der Marlenichen
   sucht alle meine Benichen,
   bindet sie in ein seiden Tuch,

gone, the juniper tree was as it had been before, and the cloth with the bones was gone. But Marleenken felt quite lighthearted and happy, just as if her brother were still alive. Then she went most happily back into the house to the table and ate.

But the bird flew away and perched on a goldsmith's house, and began to sing:

"My mother, she did slaughter me,
my father, he devoured me,
my sister, Marleenken,
gathered together all my bones,
wrapped them in a cloth of silk,
laid them beneath the juniper tree.
Kywitt, kywitt, what a beautiful bird I am!"

The goldsmith was sitting in his workshop making a golden chain, when he heard the bird that sat on his roof and sang, and this seemed so beautiful to him. Then he got up, and as he stepped over the threshold, he lost a slipper. But he went right into the middle of the street, wearing one slipper and one sock: he had his leather apron on, and in one hand he held the golden chain and in the other his tongs; and the sun shone very brightly on the street. There he stood, and looked at the bird. "Bird," he then said, "how beautifully you sing! Sing me that piece once more." "No," said the bird, "I do not sing twice for nothing. Give me the golden chain, then I will sing it once more for you." "There," said the goldsmith, "that golden chain is for you, now sing me that once more." Then the bird came and took the golden chain in his right claw, and went and sat before the goldsmith, and sang:

"My mother, she did slaughter me,
my father, he devoured me,
my sister, Marleenken,
gathered together all my bones,
wrapped them in a cloth of silk,
laid them beneath the juniper tree.
Kywitt, kywitt, what a beautiful bird I am!"

Then the bird flew away to a shoemaker, and perched on his roof, and sang:

"My mother, she did slaughter me,
my father, he devoured me,
my sister, Marleenken,

legts unter den Machandelbaum.
Kywitt, kywitt, wat vör'n schöön Vagel bün ik!'
De Schooster höörd dat un leep vör syn Döhr in Hemdsaarmels, un seeg na syn Dack un mussd de Hand vör de Ogen hollen, dat de Sünn em nich blend't. 'Vagel,' secht he, 'wat kannst du schöön singen.' Do rööp he in syn Döhr henin 'Fru, kumm mal heruut, dar is een Vagel: süh mal den Vagel, de kann maal schöön singen.' Do rööp he syn Dochter un Kinner un Gesellen, Jung un Maagd, un se kömen all up de Strat un seegen den Vagel an wo schöön he wöör, un he hadd so recht rode un gröne Feddern, un üm den Hals wöör dat as luter Gold, un de Ogen blünken em im Koop as Steern. 'Vagel,' sägd de Schooster, 'nu sing my dat Stück nochmaal.' 'Ne,' secht de Vagel, 'twemaal sing ik nich umsünst, du mußt my wat schenken.' 'Fru,' säd de Mann, 'gah na dem Bähn: up dem bäwelsten Boord door staan een Poor rode Schö, de bring herünn.' Do güng de Fru hen un hahl de Schö. 'Door, Vagel,' säd de Mann, 'nu sing my dat Stück nochmaal.' Do köhm de Vagel un nöhm de Schö in de linke Klau, un flöög wedder up dat Dack un süng

'mein Mutter der mich schlacht,
mein Vater der mich aß,
mein Schwester der Marlenichen
sucht alle meine Benichen,
bindet sie in ein seiden Tuch,
legts unter den Machandelbaum.
Kywitt, kywitt, wat vör'n schöön Vogel bün ik!'

Un as he uutsungen hadd, so flöög he wech: de Kede hadd he in de rechte un de Schö in de linke Klau, un he flöög wyt wech na ene Mähl, un de Mähl güng 'klippe klappe, klippe klappe, klippe klappe.' Un in de Mähl door seeten twintig Mählenburßen, de hauden enen Steen un hackden 'hick hack, hick hack, hick hack,' un de Mähl güng 'klippe klappe, klippe klappe, klippe klappe.' Do güng de Vagel up enen Lindenboom sitten, de vör de Mähl stünn und süng

'mein Mutter der mich schlacht,'
do höörd een up,
'mein Vater der mich aß,'
do höörden noch twe up un höörden dat,
'mein Schwester der Marlenichen'
do höörden wedder veer up,
'sucht alle meine Benichen,

> gathered together all my bones,
> wrapped them in a cloth of silk,
> laid them beneath the juniper tree.
> Kywitt, kywitt, what a beautiful bird I am!"

The shoemaker heard that and ran out of the door in his shirt sleeves, and looked at his roof, and had to hold his hand before his eyes so that the sun would not blind him. "Bird," he said, "how beautifully you sing." Then he called in at his door: "Wife, come outside for a moment, there's a bird: look at that bird, it surely sings beautifully." Then he called his daughter and her children, and his journeyman, his apprentice, and his maid, and they all came onto the street and looked at the bird: how beautiful he was; and he had such fine red and green feathers, and around his neck everything was like gold, and the eyes sparkled in his head like stars. "Bird," said the shoemaker, "now sing me that piece once more." "No," said the bird, "I do not sing twice for nothing, you must give me something." "Wife," said the man, "go to the attic: on the top shelf there stands a pair of red shoes, bring those down." Then the wife went there and fetched the shoes. "There, bird," said the man, "now sing me that piece once more." Now the bird came and took the shoes in his left claw, and flew back onto the roof, and sang:

> "My mother, she did slaughter me,
> my father, he devoured me,
> my sister, Marleenken,
> gathered together all my bones,
> wrapped them in a cloth of silk,
> laid them beneath the juniper tree.
> Kywitt, kywitt, what a beautiful bird I am!"

And when he had finished singing, he flew away; in his right claw he had the chain and in his left the shoes, and he flew far away to a mill, and the mill went "klipp klapp, klipp klapp, klipp klapp." And in the mill, there sat twenty miller's men, and they were hewing a stone, and chipping away "hick hack, hick hack, hick hack," and the mill went "klipp klapp, klipp klapp, klipp klapp." Then the bird placed himself on a lime tree, which stood before the mill, and sang:

> "My mother, she did slaughter me,"

now one stopped,

> "my father, he devoured me,"

now two more stopped and listened to that,

>   *bindet sie in ein seiden Tuch,'*
> nu hackden noch man acht,
>   *'legts unter'*
> nu noch man fyw,
>   *'den Machandelbaum.'*
> nu noch man een.
>   *'Kywitt, kywitt, wat vör'n schöön Vagel bün ik!'*

Do hüll de lezte ook up un hadd dat lezte noch höörd. 'Vagel,' secht he, 'wat singst du schöön! laat my dat ook hören, sing my dat nochmaal.' 'Ne,' secht de Vagel, 'twemaal sing ik nich umsünst, gif my den Mählensteen, so will ik dat nochmaal singen 'Ja,' secht he, 'wenn he my alleen tohöörd, so schullst du em hebben.' 'Ja,' säden de annern, 'wenn he nochmaal singt, so schall he em hebben.' Do köhm de Vagel herünn, un de Möllers saat'n all twintig mit Böhm an un böhrden Steen up, 'hu uh uhp, hu uh uhp, hu uh uhp!' Do stöök de Vagel den Hals döör dat Lock un nöhm em üm as enen Kragen, un flöög wedder up den Boom un süng

>   *'mein Mutter der mich schlacht,*
>   *mein Vater der mich aß,*
>   *mein Schwester der Marlenichen*
>   *sucht alle meine Benichen,*
>   *bindet sie in ein seiden Tuch,*
>   *legts unter den Machandelbaum.*
>   *Kywitt, kywitt, wat vör'n schöön Vagel bün ik!'*

Un as he dat uutsungen hadd, do deed he de Flünk von eenanner, un hadd in de rechte Klau de Kede un in de linke de Schö un üm den Hals den Mählensteen, un floog wyt wech na synes Vaders Huse.

In de Stuw seet de Vader, de Moder un Marleenken by Disch, un de Vader säd 'ach, wat waart my licht, my is recht so good to Mode.' 'Nä,' säd de Moder, 'my is recht so angst, so recht as wenn en swoor Gewitter kummt.' Marleenken awerst seet un weend un weend, da köhm de Vagel anflegen, un as he sik up dat Dack sett't, 'ach,' säd de Vader, 'my is so recht freudig un de Sünn schynt buten so schöön, my is recht, as schull ik enen olen Bekannten weddersehn.' 'Ne,' säd de Fru, 'my is so angst, de Täne klappern my, un dat is my as Führ in den Adern.' Un se reet sik ehr Lyfken up un so mehr, awer Marleenken seet in en Eck un weend, un hadd eren Platen vör de Ogen, un weend den Platen ganß meßnatt. Do sett't sik de Vagel up den Machandelboom un süng

> "my sister, Marleenken,"

now four more stopped,

> "gathered together all my bones,
> wrapped them in a cloth of silk,"

now there were still eight men left chipping away,

> "laid them beneath,"

now still five men,

> "the juniper tree."

now still one man.

> "Kywitt, kywitt, what a beautiful bird I am!"

Now the last one also stopped and still heard the last words. "Bird," he said, "how beautifully you sing! Let me also hear that, sing that once more for me." "No," said the bird, "I do not sing twice for nothing, give me the millstone, then I will sing it once more." "Yes," he said, "if it belonged to me alone, you could have it." "Yes," said the others, "if he sings once more, he shall have it." Now the bird came down, and the twenty millers all got hold of a beam and raised the stone, "hu uh upp, hu uh upp, hu uh upp!" Then the bird stuck his neck through the hole, and wore the stone like a collar, and flew back on the tree, and sang:

> "My mother, she did slaughter me,
> my father, he devoured me,
> my sister, Marleenken,
> gathered together all my bones,
> wrapped them in a cloth of silk,
> laid them beneath the juniper tree.
> Kywitt, kywitt, what a beautiful bird I am!"

And when he had finished singing that, he spread his wings, and had in his right claw the chain, and in his left the shoes, and around his neck the millstone, and he flew far away to his father's house.

In the room the father, the mother, and Marleenken were sitting at the table, and the father said: "Ah, how lighthearted, how very happy I feel!" "No," said the mother, "I am so frightened, just as if a heavy thunderstorm were approaching." But Marleenken sat there and wept and wept, and then the bird came flying, and when he perched on the roof, the father said: "Ah, I feel so happy, and outside the sun is shining so beautifully, I feel just as if I were going to see an old acquaintance again." "No," said the wife, "I am so

>'mein Mutter der mich schlacht,'

Do hüll de Moder de Oren to un kneep de Ogen to, un wull nich sehn un hören, awer dat bruusde ehr in de Oren as de allerstaarkste Storm, un de Ogen brennden ehr un zackden as Blitz.

> 'mein Vater der mich aß,'

'Ach, Moder,' secht de Mann, 'door is en schöön Vagel, de singt so herrlich, de Sünn schynt so warm, un dat rückt als luter Zinnemamen.'

> 'mein Schwester der Marlenichen'

Do lüd Marleenken den Kopp up de Knee un weend in eens wech, de Mann awerst säd 'ik ga henuut, ik mutt den Vagel dicht by sehn.' 'Ach, gah nich,' säd de Fru, 'my is as beewd dat ganße Huus un stünn in Flammen.' Awerst de Mann güng henuut un seeg den Vagel an

> 'sucht alle meine Benichen,
> bindt sie in ein seiden Tuch,
> legts unter den Machandelbaum.
> Kywitt, kywitt, wat vör'n schöön Vagel bün ik!'

Mit des leet de Vagel de gollne Kede fallen, un se feel dem Mann jüst um'n Hals, so recht hier herüm, dat se recht so schöön passd. Do güng he herin un säd 'süh, wat is dat vör'n schöön Vagel, heft my so 'ne schöne gollne Kede schenkd, un süht so schöön uut.' De Fru awerst wöör so angst, un füll langs in de Stuw hen, un de Mütz füll ehr von dem Kopp. Do süng de Vagel wedder

> 'mein Mutter der mich schlacht,'

'Ach, dat ik dusend Föder ünner de Eeerd wöör, dat ik dat nich hören schull!'

> 'mein Vater der mich aß,'

Do füll de Fru vör dood nedder.

> 'mein Schwester der Marlenichen'

'Ach,' säd Marleenken, 'ik will ook henuut gahn un sehn of de Vagel my wat schenkt?' Do güng se henuut.

> 'sucht alle meine Benichen,
> bindt sie in ein seiden Tuch,'

Do smeet he ehr de Schöh herünn.

> 'legts unter den Machandelbaum.
> Kywitt, kywitt, wat vör'n schöön Vagel bün ik!'

Do wöör ehr so licht un frölich. Do truck se de neen roden Schö an, un danßd un sprüng herin. 'Ach,' säd se, 'ick wöör so trurig, as ik henuut güng, un nu

frightened, my teeth are chattering, and it feels like fire in my veins." And she tore open her bodice, and still more of her clothing, but Marleenken sat in a corner and wept, and held her apron in front of her eyes and wept till it was soaking wet. Now the bird perched on the juniper tree and sang:

"My mother, she did slaughter me,"

—at that the mother covered her ears, and shut her eyes, and she wanted neither to see nor to hear, but it roared in her ears like the most powerful storm, and her eyes burned and flashed like lightning.

"My father, he devoured me,"

"Ah, mother," says the man, "that is a beautiful bird, he is singing so wonderfully; the sun is shining so warmly, and it smells here just like cinnamon."

"My sister, Marleenken,"

—at that Marleenken put her head on her knees, and wept and wept, but the man said: "I am going outside, I must see the bird close." "Ah, do not go," said the wife, "I feel as if the whole house were shaking and going up in flames." But the man went outside and looked at the bird.

"Gathered together all my bones,
wrapped them in a cloth of silk,
laid them beneath the juniper tree.
Kywitt, kywitt, what a beautiful bird I am!"

With that, the bird let the golden chain fall, and it fell exactly around the man's neck, so perfectly around that it fit beautifully. Then he went inside and said: "Look, what a beautiful bird that is, he has given me such a beautiful golden chain, and he looks so beautiful." But the wife was very frightened and fell down flat on the floor in the room, and her cap fell off her head. Now the bird sang again:

"My mother, she did slaughter me,"

—"Ah, if only I were a thousand feet beneath the earth so that I would not hear that!"

"My father, he devoured me,"

—now the wife fell down as if dead.

"My sister, Marleenken,"

"Ah," said Marleenken, "I, too, want to go outside and see if the bird will give me something." Then she went outside.

"Gathered together all my bones,
wrapped them in a cloth of silk,"

is my so licht, dat is maal en herrlichen Vagel, hett my en Poor rode Schö schenkd.' 'Ne,' säd de Fru un sprüng up, un de Hoor stünnen ehr to Baarg as Führsflammen, 'my is as schull de Welt ünnergahn, ik will ook henuut, of my lichter warden schull.' Un as se uut de Döhr köhm, bratsch! smeet ehr de Vagel den Mählensteen up den Kopp, dat se ganß tomatscht wurr. De Vader un Marleenken höörden dat un güngen henuut: do güng en Damp un Flamm un Führ up von der Städ, un as dat vorby wöör, do stünn de lütje Broder door, un he nöhm synen Vader un Marleenken by der Hand, un wören all die so recht vergnöögt un gungen in dat Huus by Disch, un eeten.[47]

—now he threw down the shoes to her.

"Laid them beneath the juniper tree.

Kywitt, kywitt, what a beautiful bird I am!"

Now she felt so lighthearted and happy, and she put on the new red shoes, and danced and jumped back inside. "Ah," she said, "I was so sad when I went outside, and now I feel so lighthearted; that surely is a wonderful bird, it has given me a pair of red shoes." "No," said the wife and jumped up, and her hair stood up like flames of fire, "I feel as if the world were coming to its end, I want to go outside, too, I might feel better." And as she stepped out of the door, crunch! the bird threw the millstone down on her head so that she was completely crushed. The father and Marleenken heard that and went outside; and smoke and flames and fire were rising from that spot, and when that was over, there stood the little brother, and he took his father and Marleenken by the hand, and all three were very happy and went into the house to the table, and ate.

10

Eating and Giving Birth: "The Juniper Tree"

> This feeling running through the veins of this mystical flesh, in which each convulsion is a manner of world and another sort of birth, loses and consumes itself in the burn of erroneous oblivion.
>
> ANTONIN ARTAUD
> *Correspondance de la momie*

This tale speaks of a deep past, of something that happened "probably two thousand years ago" (101). An exploration of considerable intensity develops, imbued with a particular kind of millennial spirit. In exploring what happened a long time ago, the tale speaks of feelings. Its plot is driven by a vicious deed and its cover-up. "The Juniper Tree," however, exhibits its narrative underside. Circumstances and activities all but concealed in "The King of the Golden Mountain," "The Glass Coffin," and "Faithful Johannes" come to the fore in this fiercely revelatory tale. Time and again, the tale coalesces with the story. Dreamlike events and terrors occur in the light of day as if there were no distinctions between a world of unchecked possibilities and the imperatives of civilized conduct. Digestive and reproductive functions engender a narrative beyond and before established categorizations. A child, who at the time of his conception brings Snow White to mind, all but partakes in a process of excretion at the time of his birth, and later in his life turns into familial food. Such a story, which is further intensified by intrafamilial executions, has its chaotic qualities; but in its primordial passions it generates an affective trajectory of compelling cohesiveness. Maternal forces, dramatically split at first, converge in the end, and in between the tale develops in constant contact with the mother who dies at the beginning, and with the stepmother who is destroyed at the end. In the wake of that final moment of violence in a turbulent tale, the age-old story signals its return.

Productive Eliminations

As in "Snow White," blood in the snow suggests both conception and sorrow. The woman under the juniper tree peels herself an apple, cuts her finger, and turns "very sad," but once she says, "if only I had a child as red as blood and as white as snow," she grows "very happy" (101). The pregnancy in "The Juniper Tree" is associated with eating at its beginning, and with the digestive tract toward its joyous and fatal end. The apple the wife peels furthermore resonates with the biblical myth of sin. Yet the figure under the juniper tree does not eat the apple. In terms of this tale she holds off forever: her body's fruit begins to grow in a singular space in which storms of hunger brew on the far side of exhilaration. After one month

> the snow disappeared; two months, and now everything was green; three months, and now the flowers came out of the ground; four months, and now all the trees grew wider, and all the green branches were intertwined; now the little birds sang so that the whole forest resounded, and the blossoms fell from the trees; and now the fifth month had passed, and she stood under the juniper tree: it smelled so beautifully, and now her heart leapt for joy, and she fell down on her knees and was beside herself with jubilation... (101)

In "röök so schön" (100)—in the Pomeranian and Hamburgian dialects of the tale[48]—a sensory and sensual perception is associated with beauty. A song's beauty will later play a crucial role. As beauty appears and stillness sets in, the woman's growth and pregnancy approaches its turning point. In the seventh month, "she snatched at the juniper berries and ate them most greedily, and now she became sad and sick..." (101). The tale had not presented the eating of the apple; the juniper berries are engorged in vivid detail. A heightened intensity and an imbalance constellate around eating as the time of birth draws near. Sin and abstinence in the image of the apple are followed by greedy ingestion and its consequences. A stream of tears pervades the story to come. A procreative and digestive cluster forms, in which the son to be born, the berries ingested and excreted, the son eaten and transformed, and the incessantly flowing tears interact with each other and with the apple that appeared on the verge of being eaten. Highlighting the tale's title, the juniper berry's diuretic properties loom large in the excesses and symptoms of the narration at hand.

Growth and abstinence are associated here, as well as overeating and elimination. When the time of birth has come, the bearer of the process is eliminated herself.[49] The mother loses her life at the time of birth, but the story in its prefigurative cast has her dying begin at conception and accelerate with final force once the juniper berries have been engorged. Throughout his history, the child develops under the sway of elimination. His birth proceeds from the abdomen in which the berries did their work. Birth and death, incipience and disposal are intimately intertwined. In yet another intensification of this semantic cluster, the mother wishes to be buried under the tree whose fruit engendered her illness.

Although the story of the tree and the newly born boy begins to take its course once the mother has died, she remains the mother in and of the tale. The multiple meanings created in the course of her conception and pregnancy unfold throughout the narrative. In contradistinction to most other tales collected by the Grimms, "The Juniper Tree" exhibits a pervasive trauma. The underlying stories in "The Glass Coffin," "The King of the Golden Mountain," and in "Faithful Johannes" speak in the intralinguistic idiom of each respective tale. More radically conceived, "The Juniper Tree" exposes its narrative entrails. The plot thereby does not move into a dominant position. Time and again, images of multiple significance and narrative progression fuse, and a broadly allusive lyric poetry appears in decisive passages. Marking clusters of condensation within an already densely significant flow of images, this poetry further contributes to a poignant presence of times past.

The new father "began to weep a lot" (101). Having buried his wife under the juniper tree, he joins the flow that had originated in her eyes, and—through the blood of conception—in the finger she had cut. He stands at the beginning of the newly evolving story, but nevertheless partakes in the dynamics that had set in with his wife.

The cluster of images from which the story takes off reverberates with her imprint on that white surface. Her finger, from which blood drips onto the snow, does not suggest conception alone. In the fruit she peels, the impetus and the digestive inversion that give rise to the narrative constellate inseparably: the mother's originative presence dissolves in its very fruitfulness.

Affective Underground

In the new family, the stepson does not fare well. Whereas in "The King of the Golden Mountain" commercial motivations poison familial life in hardly acknowledged ways, the stepmother's motivations in "The Juniper Tree" appear with graphic clarity: wishing to pass on the entire inheritance to her daughter, she tyrannizes her stepson, "so that the poor child always lived in fear" (103). "The Juniper Tree" exposes its affective underground.

Densely charged with delightful as well as deadly associations, the stepmother's apple connects with both this boy, who was conceived in the wake of a peeling, and with "de Böse" (102), "the Evil One." In a language attuned to dissociations and splittings into good and evil, "de Böse" invades the stepmother, "as if"—"as wenn" (102)—she were no longer in control of her deeds. The decisive switch into the evil mode occurs once the dialogue between mother and daughter ceases: the former looks out of the window. Seeing prevails at the time of early experience, as in "The King of the Golden Mountain," "The Glass Coffin," and—most strikingly—in "Faithful Johannes." "De Böse" arises in a splitting before language and a firmly structured sense of identity:

> And when she saw from the window that he was coming, it was just as if the Evil One overcame her, and she snatched at the apple and took it away from her daughter, and said: "You shall not have one before your brother." (103)

In its dialect form, the stepmother's look includes a relationship to the seeming truth of perception: "Un as se uut dat Fenster wohr wurr dat he köhm, so wöör dat recht, as wenn..." (102). Looking out of the window, the woman becomes aware: "wohr wurr," with its connection to what is "true," "wahr." In a sliding from "wohr" via "wurr" to the subjunctive context of "wöör," her look at the stepson partakes both in a perceptually apparent truth and the dissociative imbalance in which the one called evil takes hold of her. An overwhelming experience is linked with vision in the manner of early, prelinguistic childhood. Seeing rather than speaking, the stepmother returns to feelings from "a long time ago" (101).

Having taken away the apple from her daughter in a gesture that recalls early times of impulse and voracity, this driven figure is ready to act. Speaking with friendly words, and with eyes that radiate with the intensity of evil, she approaches the little boy with the question Snow White has to contend with in her tale: "My son, do you want to have an apple?" The boy notices the split: "Mother...how grisly you look! Yes, give me an apple" (103). Rather than staying with his visual perception, however, the boy at this crucial moment responds on a linguistic level. Coming home from school, he seems to communicate agreeably, reasonably.

The apple here and the maternal one from which he came, however, share a double, prerational message. Both alluring and deadly, the stepmother's apple recalls that of the dead mother, which in its own way had been attractive as well as fatal. From the realm of that former apple the boy's life sprang. Yet the blood in the snow and the cut finger also mark the beginning of his mother's end. In the double nature of the new apple, the boy's past comes alive. In accepting his stepmother's offer, he comes into contact with the figure at his origins.

Language as used by this stepmother lures the boy into a speechless depth. She feels as if she should "encourage him," "em toreden" (102), with its reference to "reden," "to talk." Approaching him in terms of the medium that connects with his present tasks as a schoolboy, she creates a linguistic cover that turns out to be deceptive: "And as the little boy bent into the chest, the Evil One swayed her, and crunch! she slammed the lid shut so that his head flew off and fell among the red apples" (103).

Among the apples, the boy is in his mother's proximity again, close to the death she suffered in the wake of peeling her apple. In his demise, he escapes his stepmother's reign. If the tale does not end here, it is because there is much life in this development. In falling into the apple chest, the boy's head also reapproaches the womb whence he as well as the story sprang. Digestive processes reenter the tale. As the boy becomes the protagonist of a newly invigorated story, mother's implied abstinence, her greedy and fatal swing to the other extreme, and her creatively charged eliminations return in their familial context. The stepmother's deed does not reflect on her alone. In sending the boy back to his maternal origins, she reintroduces the first mother's intense preoccupations. The stepmother's pecuniary drive is but a weak reflection of the "greedily" (101) devoured juniper berries. Her forerunner lives on in the newly developing work.

These dynamics recall the tensions between the world of the merchant in "The King of the Golden Mountain" and that of his son, whose new story takes off once he has endured the cutting off of his head, an act that in turn anticipates his dictatorial megalomania in which all heads must fall. Severed heads in "The King of the Golden Mountain" and "The Juniper Tree" evoke early events, but they also propel the respective stories toward a dinstinctly novel, if in the end prefigured terrain.

Intrafamilial Cannibalism and Avian Poetry

In the postcataclysmic narrative of "The Juniper Tree," the stepmother covers up her deed with a white cloth around her stepson's neck. Underneath, his severed head sits on his body. Once again the narrative arrives in the realm of the apple: following her mother's recommendation, Marleenken slaps her brother in the face to make him respond; his head comes to rest among the apples. A prescient silence ensues: lodged among the fruits that recall the first mother, he and his story do not yet speak.

Familial bodies and flows come to the fore all the more distinctly. Ingestion, tears, and intrafamilial cannibalism create a sense of raw drama and odd expectation. The stepmother and her daughter make a stew out of the boy. Reminiscent of the tale's first parents, Marleenken now weeps, "and all of her tears fell into the pot, and no salt at all was needed" (105). The father feasts on the stew. The stepmother explains his son's absence with a visit to his dead mother's great-uncle. In misinforming the father, she places the son in the familial neighborhood of the mother toward whom he has, in terms of the underlying story, indeed departed. Again "The Juniper Tree" presses for insight in the midst of the foreground plot. The father develops an appetite for the stew that speaks both of his son and of his first wife's engorgement of the juniper berries. Cannibalism, incest, and consumptive memory merge in this feast. As he eats his son, the father "feels as if all of it were mine" (105).

However, the tale continues to insist on its maternal beginnings. Father does not keep the son's remains in his possession, and Marleenken once again serves as the conduit of narrative change. Beginning to atone for what she believes she has done to the head underneath her mother's wrappings, she picks up the bones the father has thrown under the table and places them at the dead mother's final resting place, the juniper tree. Early scenes and movements now return. Marleenken stops crying as the mother did once she had arranged for her impending burial under the juniper tree. Her son's birth and the tale of his suffering had followed. Now the newly conceived story is about to begin.

A bird rises from the tree. Indications are that this is Marleenken's stepbrother: the cloth with the bones is gone, and she feels "as if her brother were still alive" (107). Marleenken returns to the house, sits down at the table, and eats: the tale reaches a digestive equilibrium from which it may proceed with renewed vigor. The brother, whose story now enters into its second configuration, appears both in the airy space of imagination and in an immediately present narrative. The song the bird sings is precise in its emotional tone and narrative implications. It tells of murder, incestuous cannibalism, and the gathering of bones. It also includes the juniper tree with the bones underneath. The mother who "did slaughter me" (107) emerges at the song's beginning; the mother who rests under the juniper tree partakes in its end.

In the final line, the song's creation, and that of the tale overall, resonates: "Kywitt, kywitt, wat vör'n schöön Vagel bün ik!" "Schöön" also renders the beauty of the song (106), of the stepmother's apple

(102), and of the cannibalistic meal's taste (104), as well as the beauty of the first mother (100) and of the juniper tree's enticing smell (100). Like the tale, the beautiful bird arises from a sphere of eating and, conceivably, of transformational elimination: not only ashes come to mind with this phoenix-like creature who emerges out of the juniper tree's mist and fire:[50]

> My mother, she did slaughter me,
> my father, he devoured me,
> my sister, Marleenken,
> gathered together all my bones,
> wrapped them in a cloth of silk,
> laid them beneath the juniper tree.
> Kywitt, kywitt, what a beautiful bird I am! (107)

The theme of beauty, freed from its painful connections for the moment, enters into the tale's foreground: closer to his mother than after his first birth, the boy, now bird, is a wondrous creation. In his range, words and things acquire a new radiance. As in the course of the pregnancy, when the snow melted and the woods resounded, the world comes alive.

Struck by the song's beauty, the goldsmith in his work connects with the song outside both in his awareness and through the narrative's linguistic embodiment. As he "was sitting"—"seet" (106)—in his workshop, he "heard" the bird who "seet" on his roof, and this "seemed so beautiful," "schöön" (106), to him. The world outside takes the work inside—to which it is related through word repetition and sentence structure—to a new level, which in turn brings back the tale's pregnant beginnings.

Not one to fly off into a land of sheer beauty and unfettered imagination, the bird displays a clear understanding of the exchange between goods and services. Different from his stepmother, and also from the father in "The King of the Golden Mountain," he imbues this mechanism with an air of cleverness and even humor: "'No,' said the bird, 'I do not sing twice for nothing. Give me the golden chain, then I will sing it once more for you'" (107). Having received the chain, the bird manages to strike the same chord with the shoemaker.

The red shoes the bird obtains link with the "slipper"—"Tüffel" (106)—the goldsmith loses in crossing the threshold. Shoes both stay behind and—at the end of the tale—reappear in apocalyptic circumstances. Like the "Toffel" (10) in "The King of the Golden Mountain," "Tüffel" is akin to "Teufel," "devil." In "The Juniper Tree," the story of the bird in the end does not exclude the "Evil One" (103) who makes the stepmother commit the crime. Just as the song encompasses vast spaces of human experience, its singer connects with a cohesive and wide-ranging sense of reality. His journey will take such cohesiveness toward its limits.

Uniquely combined, artistic imagination and clever realism enter into zones of memory and trauma that in the other tales do not coalesce around a common thread: the different narratives simultaneously presented in "The King of the Golden Mountain," "The Glass Coffin," and "Faithful Johannes" remain separated from each other. In the complexly self-referential world of "The Juniper Tree," the development of one thread takes a conspicuous turn toward the literal with the transfer of the bones to the juniper tree. Marleenken "tied" them up in her "best silk cloth" (105). In other renderings of the tale, the bones are lined up on a yarn and hung out of the attic. In several Hessian versions, they are linked with a thread of red silk.[51] The "golden chain" (107) acquired by the bird ties into this context as well.

Exuding a near-emblematic confidence, the bird proudly displays his new belongings: "in his right claw he had the chain and in his left the shoes, and he flew far away to a mill..." (109). The curious sound emanating from this mill creates a lyrical presence reminiscent of the many-layered song. Again, the narrative presents its memory cohesively rather than in forms of splitting. The sounds of the mill do not tell another, underlying story, but the one the song just reannounced in its first line: "My mother, she did slaughter me..." (109).

The close relationship between the bird's singing and his environment continues, evoking the intimate link between his mother's pregnancy and the nature around her. On the way to his rebirth, the bird sings what is on his mind: "My mother, she did slaughter me," whereupon one of the men stops working. The presence of memory embodied in this poetically condensed and suggestive language is further heightened in an emphasis on hearing. With phonetic immediacy, the song's reception by the next two men involves "höörden" (108), which connects both with hearing and with the work stoppage captured in "höörden...up" (108), "ceased" to work.

Through the language in which the bird's journey materializes, the narrative achieves its singular cohesion. The maternal process that brought the son, now bird, into the world reverberates throughout the tale, most graphically in activities of eating and multivalent elimination. The newly emergent protagonist's final repeat performance is tied to a stone that crushes grain on its way to ingestion. The large millstone he wishes to wear like a collar is heavy with narrative implications, as it is literally for the twenty men needed for its hoisting; yet the protagonist wears the stone lightly. It is now his stone, not a burden but an integral part of the tale that begins close to his origins. The devil suggested in the red shoes, the thread around the bones of death and life in its association with the golden chain, and the stone are all part of one development: as the bird acquires the various pieces, his journey approaches its climactic ending.

The stone in "The Juniper Tree" does not reveal its destination lightly. Chaotic, extreme circumstances appear in its path. The tale demands to be received as it unfolds dramatically in a process that for the moment defies efforts at cohesion. Events flare up with erratic force before they finally reconfigure in the narrative's overall context.

Fatal Fruitfulness

The stepmother's terror feels as if "a heavy thunderstorm" (111) were approaching. The bird is landing on the roof, the father feels happy, Marleenken weeps. The scenes and the moods from the time of the murder echo in the father and the sister, but the stepmother commences a journey into the inner and simultaneously outer reality she has previously held at bay. She is on her way to the past in which she is implicated: within her head, the chattering, "klappern" (110), of her teeth resonates with the action, the *zuklappen* through which she had chopped off her stepson's head. Similarly, the "fire" (113) in her veins places the force of evil, which she had split off from herself, into her body.

On the verge of disintegration, this haunted figure is no longer able to transform the sounds she receives into the song they would constitute. Attempting to shut out the song and the bird, the stepmother "covered her ears, and shut her eyes...but it roared in her ears like the most powerful storm, and her eyes burned and flashed like lightning" (113). The song's poetic fury intensifies in her head, which in turn emits signals of distress and turbulence.

Although the stepmother's transmutation takes the tale into apocalyptic terrain where she feels "as if the world were coming to its end" (115), her fate remains within the narrative context. The evolution of the maternal body and the year at the beginning is followed by a downward trajectory toward the end of the tale. The stepmother not only falls down "flat on the floor," but furthermore wishes for an occurrence akin to a reverse pregnancy, if the tale's initial developments reverberate at this point: "Ah, if only I were a thousand feet beneath the earth" (113), she exclaims caught in the song's evocation of horror.

The bird's message to the stepmother concerns the entire narrative. In the process leading to her death, the genesis both of the protagonist and of the tale resounds. When the bird drops the golden chain so that it falls around the father's neck, the stepmother is horror-struck. Major ingredients of the story enter into her brain; her "cap" (113) falls down at this moment, removing yet another layer of protection. Her eyes are bound to see what is put before them: "Look, what a beautiful bird that is, he has given me such a beautiful golden chain, and he looks so beautiful" (113). The threefold repetition of "beautiful" creates a distinct verbal field, bringing back one more time the theme through which the narrative and its protagonist, in his various configurations, acquire much of their presence and cohesiveness.

The tale does not relent. Upon receiving the red shoes from the bird, Marleenken displays them to her mother, who jumps to her feet as if the devil in these shoes and from her evil deed had come alive. In the narrative's explosively charged space, the stepmother's individual presence hardly matters any more. About to be eliminated from the tale, she is nevertheless irrevocably enmeshed with its visions. She, too, is hardly part of another story in this consistently cohesive narrative; to the end, she remains tied to the images and processes that characterize the tale's overall course. Her tormented, driven figure ends up near the first mother.[52]

In a final turn, the drama of the stepmother's reverse development is rewritten, if only for a brief interlude. Her body takes on the life of the shoes, "and her hair stood up like flames of fire" (115), reminiscent of the flame that shot up out of the juniper tree—the mother's burial site—when the son was reborn. In the figures of the "good" and the "bad" mother, notions of good and evil come together closely.

With her hair rising like flames, the stepmother's appearance approaches representations of the Holy Spirit. The stepmother is vastly evocative in this final phase; having wished to be deep in the earth, she also conjures up the heights of heaven. She is the impossible heroine in an ineffable configuration of universal scope and depth. In her final metamorphosis, knowledge and imagination flare up at outer limits of narrative embodiment—and of early memory.

In the tale's final sentences, the stepmother steps into an ever-elusive, primordial realm: "I feel as if the world were coming to its end, I want to go outside, too, I might feel better" (115). The end of which she speaks issues from the stone. At the moment at which it reaches her head, the stepmother and the tale coalesce in a primal bang that reverberates in countless stories to be told thereafter: "And as she stepped out of the door, crunch! the bird threw the millstone down on her head so that she was completely crushed" (115). At once the tale transmits that sound to a space beyond its beginnings: "crunch!"— "bratsch!"—engenders "crushed," "tomatscht" (114).

The stepmother's death underneath the stone marks the son's rebirth. She is his mother now, in fatal fruitfulness, as is his first mother from the tale's beginning. At this moment, the two maternal figures are no longer split off from each other. Once he has disposed of his stepmother, the bird is transformed back into the human son, in a birth recalling the flames that rose from her head a few moments ago. Coinciding with her destruction, the son is being born in an immediate consequence of "bratsch!" and "tomatscht": "smoke and flames and fire were rising from that spot, and when that was over, there stood the little brother..." (115).

The protagonist seems beyond the age of splitting now. He has moved through the turbulent early times of the story and emerged from the thread that bound his bones. He picks up the narrative thread by taking his father and his sister, Marleenken, by the hand, and all three "were very happy." Yet their story ends with a glaring absence at the table where they—with the last word of the tale—"ate" (115).[53] They do what the "good" mother did not do, then overdid at the beginning, and what the "bad" mother offered at the site of the chest; but neither is there now in the little family's happiness. Once again eating is permeated by an imbalance. The two mother figures had connected in culinary ways all along: the early mother stopped short of eating the apple, then engorged the berries and released the son from her body; the later one made the son's severed head fall among the apples in the chest, then produced the bloody stew, and in her own way engendered a second journey toward birth. In its productive eliminations, the story goes on.

11

Ending

> ...sooner or later, people will realize that the curtain adorned with pretty social models is a cheat.
>
> CZESLAW MILOSZ
> *Ziemia Ulro*

Throughout these pages, happy endings met with distrust. The foreground plot does not tell the story. Different from received interpretations, but consonant with recent critiques of developmentalism and of linear, chronological depictions of childhood, the present study does not undertake to construct a psychological sense through which the Grimms' tales would speak in the service of cultural consolidations. Neither a particular child with specific tasks in a game of achievement and accommodation nor an adult who would know about such a child emerges here. Rather something felt and told pervades thoughts and perceptions that in the end refuse to harden on behalf of a singularly defined protagonist. Passions and sufferings of formation, attachment, and of sheer survival move these narratives in their precise, yet semiotically agile perambulations.

Regarded closely, these opaque texts, which from developmentalist points of view are cast as classifiable tales of childhood, turn out to be exceedingly complex: they expose a silence at the core of established cogitation and self-assured assertiveness. Such narratives murmur of death, terror, and of a longing for containment in the midst of fragmentation and mental collapse. They take us into early realms of experience, which can be felt in their present-day reverberations, but not mapped along the lines of a retrospectively organized inquiry.

Although hidden realities seem to manifest themselves in the much-discussed, frightful substratum of the Grimms' tales, this narrative underground in its own ways conceals certain more sharply disturbing stories of destruction. For these stories, there are no words, and argumentations that claim to point out underlying horrific elements unwittingly contribute to covering up even deeper fears. To the extent that interpretations of these multilayered narratives incorporate pain and evil into a discursive language of adulthood, they add to the machinery of forgetting, cocreating a status quo in which early life has neither place nor voice. In the workings of such interpretations, the relatively accessible realm of cruelty and abuse functions anaesthetically. The plots, behaviors, and aberrations that manifest in the only slightly concealed terrain of fairy-tale infamy obscure a terrifying underworld.

The readings performed in this study strive for their intrinsic breaking points. There, it is imagined, they turn polysemous, unruly, endlessly wide. In such dynamics, close readings turn groundless, fall through layers of interpretation toward a space and time before words. In the boundary region between verbalization and preverbal experience, reading and hearing these narratives involves a process of learning between linguistic formulation and a world whose frights and promises escape one's grasp.

Viewed in terms of plot progression, the language of the Grimm narratives seems clear enough. Yet once received in their multivalent range, the words and images come alive with feelings and realizations that defy semantic containment. Anger wells up with an intensity that, as with the cutting off of heads, might be called psychotic. Such a diagnostic resonance, however, fades when the blood flows, for example, from the trunks of children beheaded by their father. A certain concealment takes place in calling these tales gruesome, or in attributing a psychotic dimension to them. A sense of falseness develops when engaging fairy-tale extremities through terminologically delimited means.

In their affective sphere, these narratives reflect experience before linguistic articulation; but the mirrors are broken. It is no coincidence that the much-quoted stepmotherly queen consults her mirror before requesting a murderous deed that in its infanticidal force destroys any semblance of a warm, maternal smile. The victim of her intent will never again be able to find herself recognized, let alone felt, in the

Ending

realm of that—with Winnicott—first mirror. If this resounds with the loss of the first mother, it evokes unspeakable events all the more. Madness and despondency as measured against conceptions of health and well-being do not apply here. The depth experience in these fairy tales does not appear within the perimeters of dualistically contrastive thought. The world of the twins, whose heads are chopped off by their father with their mother's subsequent approval, hardly interrelates with the tale of a servant's faithfulness; but it registers with an audience attuned to images and suggestions that are not admitted into the manifest body of the text.

Sufferings of the flesh all the more strongly occupy an imagination informed, but not enclosed, by fairy-tale happenings. In a space before words, boundless anger connects with sources of violence. The King of the Golden Mountain, a relative of the twins born to the Princess of the Golden Roof, endures his own head's removal before he commands that all heads fall. In the chain of events that leads to this action, the protagonist's father plays a decisive role, subjecting him to a heartless deal, kicking him into the stream, and finally refusing to acknowledge his success in life. Some concreteness thus accrues to the son's trajectory; but the family dynamics at work here undermine conceptions of familial texture. Nothing remains reliably intact between father and son, nor between the son and his own family. Familial devastation reigns in a labyrinth of narrational fissures and inflections.

Enclosure in this context at times takes on its own life upon which everything depends, but which in a realm between dream and wakefulness turns permeable. The story of the female protagonist who emerges from the glass coffin, but does not markedly evolve from her nightmarish past in her ostentatiously happy ending, remains tied to membranous configurations that do not offer her a sense of self. She does, to be sure, set out to tell her story, and she refers to her stunned silence. She also injects her anger forcefully into the tale's dealings, much like the Frog King's heroine, and in some consonance with the protagonist of the Golden Mountain who moves through silence, then bursts into furious action. Yet in firing the shot at the stranger, she kills her own horse: now she is naked, enclosed in glass, enveloped in nothing but her skin and hair. The tailor's borderline existence, dermatically inflected, matches her condition precisely. Her story remains in flux, suspended forever in the tale that ends with her wedding, in which she is drawn back toward her brother's world and that of her dead parents. The memory of an unspeakable pain lurks in this ceremonial occasion and its self-canceling context.

The fairy stories explored in this study carry memories that resist and elude signification. Such narratives resonate with early, preverbal experience. The terrors around the Juniper Tree speak with particular insistence. In their relentless physicality, they evoke depths where imagination turns real. In the strangely familiar excretions and the oral excessiveness of this narrative, a record of human catastrophe called fairy tale comes close to being known.

Notes

1 This involves a departure from developmentalist views of childhood. For critical analyses of such views cf. Erica Burman, *Deconstructing Developmental Psychology*, and Rex and Wendy Stainton Rogers, "Word Children" (1998), pp. 178–81, 201. Also cf. Stainton Rogers (1992), pp. 37–53. In "Creative Writers and Day-Dreaming," Sigmund Freud sees childhood play in primarily ahistoric terms, setting early fantasy apart from linear progression, as Lucie Armitt emphasizes in *Theorising the Fantastic* (Armitt, 4–7). Peter L. Hunt's *Criticism, Theory, and Children's Literature* remains firmly connected with defined notions of childhood development (Hunt, 87–97).

2 For particular pedagogical and ideological forces in the rendering of fairy tales cf. Ellis, pp. 94–103, McGlathery (1993), pp. 5–58, Zipes (1989), pp. 28–42, and Zipes (2000), pp. 203 f., 219.

3 Cf. Daniel N. Stern's (1985) chapter, "The Sense of a Verbal Self," pp. 162–82, as well as Adam Phillips' empathic account in *The Beast in the Nursery*, pp. 42–64. For a psychologically informed fictional presentation of early linguistic experience, cf. Stern (1990), *Diary of a Baby*, pp. 111–27. For linguistically focused research also cf. *Children's Single-Word Speech* (Martyn D. Barrett, ed.), *The Transition from Prelinguistic to Linguistic Communication* (Roberta Michnick Golinkoff, ed.), and *How Babies Talk: The Magic and Mystery of Language in the First Three Years of Life* (R. M. Golinkoff and Kathy Hirsh-Pasek).

4 Cf. Phillips' reference to bodily functions in the rise of language (*The Beast in the Nursery*, 62 f.).

5 In his classic work, *Centuries of Childhood*, Philippe Ariès exposes the notion of childhood as a sociocultural construction. Also cf. Frances G. Wickes' early analytic study, *The Inner World of Childhood*. Jacqueline Rose's exploration of children's literature in *The Case of Peter Pan* connects language and childhood in a critique of culturally reductive fantasies of origin. In her wide-ranging work, *Children's Literature*, Karín Lesnik-Oberstein (1994) creates critical spaces for fresh receptions of the literature of childhood. Also cf. her essay, "Childhood and Textuality" (1998), pp. 2–26, and "Fantasy, Childhood and Literature: In Pursuit of Wonderlands" (1999), pp. 197–200.

6 Cf. Winnicott's formulations in "Creativity and Its Origins," p. 65, and in "Mirror-Role of Mother and Family in Child Development," p. 114.

7 Lesnik-Oberstein (1994) appreciates Winnicott's "acute awareness" (Lesnik-Oberstein, 225) of pre-appropriated experience as well.

8 The texts of the tales in this study, to which my parenthetical page numbers will refer, are based on the 7th edition of the Grimms' *Kinder und Hausmärchen* [sic, no hyphen] as it appeared in 1857.—Translations mine.—The present tale appears on pp. 35-41 of vol. 2 of the Grimms' edition (tale no. 92). In contradistinction to the recent critical edition by Hans-Jörg Uther (1996), I have not altered the spelling, the size of the paragraphs, or the punctuation of the original texts. I also refrained from correcting apparent errors in these texts. Such slips, *Versehen*, are at least of documentary significance.—In all four tales, the original size of the paragraphs in-

fluences the overall rhythm perceived in listening and reading. By way of numerous new paragraphs, Uther's rendering decreases textual flow and increases structural division. In "The Juniper Tree," Uther's editorial alterations of the bird's song result in rhythmic changes of special significance: the addition of several commas interrupts the text's somewhat breathless lyric movement.—Heinz Rölleke (1980), in his edition of the 7th edition, stays close to the text, but corrects errors and modernizes spelling as well as punctuation (cf. Rölleke III, 434).—The italicization of the Grimm texts in the present volume is mine.

9 Errata in the Grimm text (left unchanged here) include: the quotation marks preceding "Da sprach er 'gerne will ich [ ]'" (8), and "'[...] nun gebt mir das Schwert'" (12), and following "hätte er nichts mehr übrig als diesen Acker" (4). Also: the missing quotation mark following "nicht mit bösem Willen" (10).

10 In my translations of the tales in this study, to which my parenthetical page numbers will refer, I pursue a linguistic closeness to the formulations in the Grimm collection. While this attention to textual specificity addresses a momentous narrative underworld, it also engages a primary "foreignness" in translation: cf. Walter Benjamin's seminal essay, "The Task of the Translator" (1923), and Lawrence Venuti's recent "Translation, Community, Utopia" (2000).—Margaret Hunt's *Grimm's [sic] Household Tales* (1884) remains near to textual specificities as well. More recent translations include Ralph Manheim's elegant, if frequently imprecise *Grimms' Tales for Young and Old* (1977), and Jack Zipes' inspired *The Complete Fairy Tales of the Brothers Grimm* (1987).

11 Cf. Julia Kristeva's recent psychoanalytic reflections on notions of the plot-oriented tale and of discourses that "blur the linearity of narration" (Kristeva, 772).

12 Regarding manifestations of violence in the Grimms' tales, cf. Maria Tatar's poignant elucidations in *The Hard Facts of the Grimms' Fairy Tales* and in *Off with Their Heads!*

13 Cf. Otto Kernberg's informative overview (Kernberg, 3–47).

14 Cf. Bruno Bettelheim's discussion of splitting in fairy tales as a childhood defense mechanism (Bettelheim, 66–70).

15 Cf. Melanie Klein, "Our Adult World and Its Roots in Infancy," pp. 248–50.

16 For confluences of creative and psychotic languages, cf. Kudszus (1978), "Reflections on the Double Bind in Literature and Psychopathology," pp. 20–29.

17 Cf. Winnicott's exploration of an intermediate area of experience in "Transitional Objects and Transitional Phenomena."

18 Attentive to stylistic and formal features without regard for intrinsic tensions and suggestive inconsistencies, Max Lüthi's investigations in *The Fairytale as Art Form and Portrait of Man* nevertheless demonstrate the fruitfulness of looking at fairy tales in their particular textual manifestations.

19 In *Postmodern Fairy Tales: Gender and Narrative Strategies*, Cristina Bacchilega considers stories springing from borderlines of traditional narratives (Bacchilega, 22 f.).

20 Cf., e.g., *Grimm's [sic] Household Tales*, trans. Margaret Hunt, vol. 2, p. 30.

21 Cf. Marie-Louise von Franz, *Shadow and Evil in Fairy Tales*, p. 80.

22 For pervasive cultural determinants of such a fury cf. the chapter "Poisonous Pedagogy" in Alice Miller's *For Your Own Good: Hidden Cruelty in Child-Rearing and the Roots of Violence.*

23 Cf. Winnicott's (1967) seminal "Mirror-Role of Mother and Family in Child Development." Also cf. his "Primary Introduction to External Reality" (Winnicott [1948], 23 f.).
24 From the 7th ed. of Jacob and Wilhelm Grimm, Kinder [sic] und Hausmärchen, Große Ausgabe: vol. 2, pp. 305-312 (tale no. 163).
25 Kudszus (1999), "The Possibility of Extremes: Skins of a Tale," forms an earlier version of this chapter.
26 Translations from this tale mine. KHM refers to Heinz Rölleke's 1980 edition.
27 Cf. Rölleke (1998), pp. 288–302. Quotes ibid., p. 294. Trans. mine.
28 Skin analysis of "The Glass Coffin" in turn connects with the psychoanalytic investigations of Didier Anzieu et al. (Anzieu 1989, 1990).
29 In his seminal article, "Autistic Shapes," Frances Tustin elucidates this "primitive" territory psychoanalytically. Also cf. Thomas H. Ogden's *The Primitive Edge of Experience*, pp. 52–56.
30 Cf. Ruth B. Bottigheimer's and A. B. Chinen's observations on subjugation and female silence in fairy tales (Bottigheimer, 71–80; Chinen, 104 f.).
31 For the incestuous quality of the relationship between the siblings, cf. James M. McGlathery (1991), pp. 43–45.
32 Cf. Winnicott's reflections on "potential space" in its seminal significance for cultural interaction ("The Place Where We Live," 107–10).
33 Cf. Hans-Jörg Uther's edition of the Grimms' tales, vol. 4, p. 304.
34 Cf. Heinz Rölleke (1993), *Grimms Märchen, wie sie nicht im Buche stehen*, p. 94. Also cf. the literary precursor to "The Glass Coffin," *Das verwöhnte Mutter-Söhngen*, which has "penetrating glances" (Rölleke [1998], 296).
35 With regard to the stranger, Bottigheimer refers to abusive elements (Bottigheimer, 159).
36 From the 7th ed. of Jacob and Wilhelm Grimm, Kinder [sic] und Hausmärchen, Große Ausgabe: vol. 1, pp. 30-38 (tale no. 6).
37 Errata in the Grimm text (left unchanged here) include: the missing quotation marks before "wenn ich nicht hineinkomme [...]" (74), and following "das schöne Bild?" (74).
38 For the epistemological range of *Versprechen* in the context of modern, twentieth-century imagination, cf. Kudszus (1981), "Versprechen, Verschreiben, Verstehen."
39 Cf. Charles Perrault, "La Barbe Bleue" (1697). Also cf. "Blaubart," "Bluebeard," tale number 62 in vol. 1 (1812) of the Grimms' 1st edition: *Kinder- und Hausmärchen*, KHM II, p. 465–68 (appendix no. 9). Rölleke's bibliographical commentary appears in KHM III, p. 525 f. Cf. furthermore "Fitchers Vogel," "Fitcher's Bird" (KHM I, 235–39).
40 Bollas, *The Shadow of the Object*, p. 4.
41 Referring to "Faithful Johannes" and other narratives, Lüthi writes of the "shock effect of beauty" as a characteristic event in fairy tales (Lüthi, 7–10).
42 For a nuanced exploration of countertransferential processes cf. Thomas Ogden, *Subjects of Analysis*, pp. 137–65.
43 For the alchemical symbol of the raven in its connection with unconscious realities, cf. Daryl Sharp, *The Secret Raven*, p. 48.
44 Ball, *Der Künstler und die Zeitkrankheit*, p. 39 f. Trans. mine.

45 Referring to Margaret Atwood's, Angela Carter's, and Jane Campion's recastings of the Bluebeard tale, Bacchilega develops a postmodern feminist potential of this narrative (Bacchilega, 104–38).
46 From the 7th ed. of Jacob and Wilhelm Grimm, *Kinder [sic] und Hausmärchen*, Große Ausgabe: vol. 1, pp. 232-241 (tale no. 47).
47 Errata in the Grimm text (left unchanged here) include: "un Marleeken [sic] weend [...]" (104); "Marleeken [sic] awerst wöör [...]" (104); the non-capitalization of "goldsmidt" (106, l. 23); the missing period and the missing quotation mark following "so will ik dat nochmaal singen" (110); and the misspelling of "Eeerd" (112).
48 Cf. Reinhold Steig, "Zur Entstehungsgeschichte der Märchen und Sagen der Brüder Grimm," pp. 279–300, and Bolte/Polívka, vol. 1, pp. 412 f. The 7th edition of the Grimms' Fairy Tales (Große Ausgabe)—on which the present study is based—contains, with very minor differences, Philipp Otto Runge's version of the tale as edited by his brother Daniel. Cf. Runge, *Hinterlassene Schriften*, vol. 1, pp. 424–29.
49 In *The Hunger Artists*, Maud Ellmann performs a lucid inquiry into the interrelationship of self-starvation and creativity.
50 As may be perceived with Norman O. Brown, *Life Against Death: The Psychoanalytical Meaning of History*. Cf. the chapter "The Excremental Vision" (Brown, 179–201).
51 For these and other versions, cf. Bolte/Polívka, vol. 1, pp. 413 f., and Michael Belgrader, p. 112.
52 With regard to fairy tales in general, Sibylle Birkhäuser-Oeri connects opposite manifestations of motherhood (Birkhäuser-Oeri, 26–28). Referring to "The Juniper Tree," Torborg Lundell points to the repressive elimination of the stepmother (Lundell, 97 f.). Also cf. Jacqueline M. Schectman's emphasis on the stepmother's point of view in her analysis of several other fairy tales.
53 In her analysis of abusive dynamics in "The Juniper Tree," Tatar (1992) notes the "eerily static" (Tatar, 226) quality of this ending.

References

Anzieu, Didier. *The Skin Ego*. Trans. Chris Turner. New Haven: Yale UP, 1989. (*Le Moi-Peau*. Paris: Bordas, 1985.)

———, ed. *Psychic Envelopes*. Trans. Daphne Briggs. London: Karnac, 1990. (*Les enveloppes psychiques*. Paris: Bordas, 1987.)

Ariès, Philippe. *Centuries of Childhood. A Social History of Family Life*. Trans. Robert Baldick. New York: Alfred A. Knopf, 1962. (*L'Enfant et la vie familiale sous l'ancien régime*. Paris: Librairie Plon, 1960.)

Armitt, Lucie. *Theorising the Fantastic*. London: Arnold, 1996.

Bacchilega, Cristina. *Postmodern Fairy Tales: Gender and Narrative Strategies*. Philadelphia: U of Pennsylvania P, 1997.

Ball, Hugo. *Der Künstler und die Zeitkrankheit. Ausgewählte Schriften*. Ed. Hans Burkhard Schlichting. Frankfurt am Main: Suhrkamp, 1984.

Barrett, Martyn D., ed. *Children's Single-Word Speech*. Chichester: John Wiley & Sons, 1985.

Belgrader, Michael. *Das Märchen von dem Machandelboom*. Frankfurt am Main: Peter Lang, 1980.

Benjamin, Walter. "The Task of the Translator" ("Die Aufgabe des Übersetzers," 1923). Trans. Harry Zohn. *The Translation Studies Reader*. Ed. Lawrence Venuti. 15–23.

Bettelheim, Bruno. *The Uses of Enchantment: The Meaning and Importance of Fairy Tales*. 1976. New York: Random House, 1989.

Birkhäuser-Oeri, Sibylle. *The Mother. Archetypal Image in Fairy Tales*. Ed. Marie-Louise von Franz. Trans. Michael Mitchell. Toronto: Inner City, 1988. (*Die Mutter im Märchen*. Stuttgart: Adolf Bonz, 1977.)

Bollas, Christopher. *The Shadow of the Object: Psychoanalysis of the Unthought Known*. London: Free Association, 1987.

Bolte, Johannes, and Georg Polívka. *Anmerkungen zu den Kinder- und Hausmärchen der Brüder Grimm*. 2nd ed. 5 vols. Hildesheim: Georg Olms, 1963.

Bottigheimer, Ruth B. *Grimms' Bad Girls and Bold Boys: The Moral and Social Vision of the Tales*. New Haven: Yale UP, 1987.

Brown, Norman O. *Life Against Death: The Psychoanalytical Meaning of History*. 1959. Middletown: Wesleyan UP, 1970.

Burman, Erica. *Deconstructing Developmental Psychology*. London and New York: Routledge, 1994.

Chinen, A. B. *Waking the World: Classic Tales of Women and the Heroic Feminine*. New York: Putnam, 1996.

Ellis, John M. *One Fairy Story Too Many: The Brothers Grimm and Their Tales*. Chicago: U of Chicago P, 1983.

Ellmann, Maud. *The Hunger Artists. Starving, Writing, and Imprisonment*. Cambridge: Harvard UP, 1993.
Franz, Marie-Louise von. *Shadow and Evil in Fairy Tales*. Irving: Spring, 1980.
Freud, Sigmund. *The Standard Edition of the Complete Psychological Works of Sigmund Freud*. Ed. James Strachey. Vol. 9. London: Hogarth, 1959.
———. "Creative Writers and Day-Dreaming." 1908. *Complete Psychological Works*. Vol. 9. 141–53.
Golinkoff, Roberta Michnick, ed. *The Transition from Prelinguistic to Linguistic Communication*. Hillsdale: Lawrence Erlbaum, 1983.
———, and Kathy Hirsh-Pasek. *How Babies Talk: The Magic and Mystery of Language in the First Three Years of Life*. New York: Penguin, 1999.
Grimm, Jacob and Wilhelm (Brüder Grimm). *Kinder [sic] und Hausmärchen*. Große Ausgabe. 7th ed. 2 vols. Göttingen: Verlag der Dieterichschen Buchhandlung, 1857.
———. *Kinder und Hausmärchen*. Vol. 3. Göttingen: Verlag der Dieterich'schen Buchhandlung, 1856.
———. *Grimm's Household Tales*. Trans. Margaret Hunt. 2 vols. 1884. Detroit: Singing Tree Press, 1968.
———. *Grimms' Tales for Young and Old*. Trans. Ralph Manheim. New York: Doubleday, 1977.
———. *Kinder- und Hausmärchen*. 3 vols. (vols. 1 and 2: Große Ausgabe. 7th ed. 1857; vol. 3: 3rd ed. 1856). Ed. Heinz Rölleke. Stuttgart: Reclam, 1980. [= KHM]
———. *The Complete Fairy Tales of the Brothers Grimm*. Trans. Jack Zipes. Toronto and New York: Bantam, 1987.
———. *Kinder- und Hausmärchen*. Ed. Hans-Jörg Uther. 4 vols. Munich: Eugen Diederichs, 1996.
Grimm, Wilhelm. "Der gläserne Sarg." 1836. *Grimms Märchen, wie sie nicht im Buche stehen*. Ed. Heinz Rölleke (1993). 89-97.
Hunt, Margaret, trans. *Grimm's Household Tales*. 2 vols. 1884. Detroit: Singing Tree Press, 1968.
Hunt, Peter L. *Criticism, Theory, and Children's Literature*. Oxford: Basil Blackwell, 1991.
Kernberg, Otto F. *Borderline Conditions and Pathological Narcissism*. New York: Aronson, 1975.
Klein, Melanie. *Envy and Gratitude and Other Works*. Ed. Roger Money-Kyrle in collaboration with Betty Joseph, Edna O'Shaughnessy, and Hanna Segal. London: Hogarth, 1980.
———. "Our Adult World and Its Roots in Infancy." 1959. *Envy and Gratitude*. 247–63.
Kristeva, Julia. "From Symbols to Flesh: The Polymorphous Destiny of Narration." *The International Journal of Psychoanalysis* 81 (2000): 771–87.
Kudszus, W. G. "Reflections on the Double Bind in Literature and Psychopathology." *Sub-Stance* (1978): 19–36.
———. "Versprechen, Verschreiben, Verstehen: Ansätze zu einer Erkenntniskritik mit Kafka." *Literaturwissenschaft und Geistesgeschichte*. Ed. Jürgen Brummack et al. Tübingen: Niemeyer, 1981. 837–46.

———. "The Possibility of Extremes: Skins of a Tale." *Interdigitations: Essays for Irmengard Rauch*. Ed. Gerald F. Carr, Wayne Harbert, and Lihua Zhang. New York: Peter Lang, 1999. 637–46.

Lesnik-Oberstein, Karín. *Children's Literature: Criticism and the Fictional Child*. Oxford: Clarendon, 1994.

———, ed. *Children in Culture: Approaches to Childhood*. London: Macmillan, 1998.

———. "Childhood and Textuality: Culture, History, Literature." 1998. *Children in Culture: Approaches to Childhood*. 1–28.

———. "Fantasy, Childhood and Literature: In Pursuit of Wonderlands." 1999. *Writing and Fantasy*. Eds. Ceri Sullivan and Barbara White. 197–206.

Lüthi, Max. *The Fairytale as Art Form and Portrait of Man*. Trans. Jon Erickson. Bloomington: Indiana UP, 1984. (*Das Volksmärchen als Dichtung: Ästhetik und Anthropologie*. Munich: Eugen Diederichs, 1975.)

Lundell, Torborg. *Fairy Tale Mothers*. New York: Peter Lang, 1990.

Manheim, Ralph, trans. *Grimms' Tales for Young and Old*. New York: Doubleday, 1977.

McGlathery, James M. *Fairy Tale Romance: The Grimms, Basile, and Perrault*. Urbana: U of Illinois P, 1991.

———. Grimms' Fairy Tales. A History of Criticism on a Popular Classic. Columbia: Camden House, 1993.

Miller, Alice. *For Your Own Good: Hidden Cruelty in Child-Rearing and the Roots of Violence*. Trans. Hildegarde and Hunter Hannum. New York: Farrar, 1983.

Ogden, Thomas H. *The Primitive Edge of Experience*. Northvale: Jason Aronson, 1989.

———. *Subjects of Analysis*. Northvale: Jason Aronson, 1994.

Perrault, Charles. "La Barbe Bleue." 1697. *Contes*. Ed. Marc Soriano. Paris: Flammarion, 1989. *Perrault's Complete Fairy Tales*. Tr. A. E. Johnson et al. New York: Dodd, Mead, 1961.

Phillips, Adam. *The Beast in the Nursery*. New York: Pantheon, 1998.

Rölleke, Heinz, ed. *Kinder- und Hausmärchen*, by Brüder Grimm. 3 vols. (vols. 1 and 2: Große Ausgabe. 7th ed. 1857; vol. 3: 3rd ed. 1856). Stuttgart: Reclam, 1980. [= KHM]

———, ed. *Grimms Märchen, wie sie nicht im Buche stehen*. Frankfurt am Main: Insel, 1993.

———. *Grimms Märchen und ihre Quellen: Die literarischen Vorlagen der Grimmschen Märchen synoptisch vorgestellt und kommentiert*. Trier: Wissenschaftlicher Verlag, 1998.

Rose, Jacqueline. *The Case of Peter Pan or The Impossibility of Children's Fiction*. London: Macmillan, 1984.

Runge, Philipp Otto. *Hinterlassene Schriften*. Ed. Daniel Runge. Vol. 1. Hamburg: Perthes, 1840.

Schectman, Jacqueline M. *The Stepmother in Fairy Tales: Bereavement and the Feminine Shadow*. Boston: Sigo, 1993.

Sharp, Daryl. *The Secret Raven: Conflict and Transformation in the Life of Franz Kafka*. Toronto: Inner City, 1980.

Stainton Rogers, Rex and Wendy. *Stories of Childhood: Shifting Agendas of Child Concern*. Toronto: U of Toronto P, 1992.

———. "Word Children." 1998. *Children in Culture: Approaches to Childhood*. Ed. Karín Lesnik-Oberstein. 1–28.

Steig, Reinhold. "Zur Entstehungsgeschichte der Märchen und Sagen der Brüder Grimm." *Archiv für das Studium der neueren Sprachen und Litteraturen* 107 (1901): 277–310.

Stern, Daniel N. *The Interpersonal World of the Infant: A View from Psychoanalysis and Developmental Psychology*. New York: Basic, 1985.

———. *Diary of a Baby*. New York: Basic, 1990.

Sullivan, Ceri, and Barbara White, eds. *Writing and Fantasy*. London: Addison Wesley Longman, 1999.

Tatar, Maria M. *The Hard Facts of the Grimms' Fairy Tales*. Princeton: Princeton UP, 1987.

———. *Off with Their Heads!: Fairy Tales and the Culture of Childhood*. Princeton: Princeton UP, 1992.

Tustin, Frances. "Autistic Shapes." *International Review of Psycho-Analysis* 11 (1984): 279–90.

Uther, Hans-Jörg, ed. *Kinder- und Hausmärchen*. 4 vols. Munich: Eugen Diederichs, 1996.

Venuti, Lawrence, ed. *The Translation Studies Reader*. London and New York: Routledge, 2000.

———. "Translation, Community, Utopia." *The Translation Studies Reader*. 468–88.

Wickes, Frances G. *The Inner World of Childhood*. 1927. Rev. ed. New York: Appleton-Century, 1966.

Winnicott, D. W. *Playing and Reality*. London and New York: Routledge, 1989 (London: Tavistock, 1971).

———. "Transitional Objects and Transitional Phenomena." *Playing and Reality*. 1–25.

———. "Creativity and Its Origins." *Playing and Reality*. 65–85.

———. "The Place Where We Live." *Playing and Reality*. 104–110.

———. "Mirror-Role of Mother and Family in Child Development." 1967. *Playing and Reality*. 111–18.

———. "Primary Introduction to External Reality: The Early Stages." 1948. *Thinking about Children*. 21–28.

Zipes, Jack, trans. *The Complete Fairy Tales of the Brothers Grimm*. Toronto and New York: Bantam, 1987.

———. *The Brothers Grimm: From Enchanted Forests to the Modern World*. London and New York: Routledge, 1989.

———, ed. *The Oxford Companion to Fairy Tales*. Oxford: Oxford UP, 2000.

Index

abandonment
  28, 29, *35*, 57, 63, *73*
abuse
  28, 91, 98, 132, *137*, *138*
adult
  2, 3, 19, 20, 22, 24, 26, 97, 131, 132, *136*
affect
  46, 54, 56, 58, 68, 88, 91, 117, 120, 132
ambiguity
  16, 46
ambivalence
  3, 28, 87, 88
anger
  3, *11*, *13*, 16, 17, 31, 98, 132, 133
Anzieu, Didier
  45, *137*
Ariès, Philippe
  135
Armitt, Lucie
  135
Artaud, Antonin
  117
Atwood, Margaret
  138
Ausländer, Rose
  1
awareness
  22, 27, 28, 45, 49, 54, 56, 58, 59, 66, 68, 89, 92, 96, 121, 124, *135*
Bacchilega, Cristina
  136, *138*
Ball, Hugo
  93, *137*
Barrett, Martyn D.
  135
beauty
  7, 9, *11*, 24, *35*, *37*, *41*, 45, 46, 52, 59, 69, *75*, *77*, *81*, 89, 90, 94, *101*, *103*, *105*, *107*, *109*, *111*, *113*, *115*, 118, 123, 124, 127, *137*
beginning
  1, 2, 3, 17, 19, 20, 24, 26, 28, 30, *37*, 46, 47, 54, 57, 60, 61, 62, 63, 64, 65, 66, 67, 68, 70, 90, 92, 93, 94, 95, 96, 97, 117, 118, 119, 121, 123, 124, 126, 127, 128, 129
Belgrader, Michael
  138
Benjamin, Walter
  136
Bettelheim, Bruno
  136
Birkhäuser-Oeri, Sibylle
  138
birth
  9, *79*, *83*, 96, 117, 118, 119, 123, 124, 125, 128, 129, 133
blood
  81, *83*, 87, 89, 94, 95, 97, 98, *101*, *103*, *105*, 118, 119, 120, 121, 129, 132
Bluebeard
  88, 89, 97, 98, *137*, *138*
body
  2, 3, *9*, 31, *35*, 46, 47, 52, 53, 54, 57, 58, 59, 65, 68, *81*, 87, 95, 118, 122, 126, 127, 128, 129, 133, *135*
Bollas
  137
Bolte
  138
borderline
  17, 57, 68, 93, 133, *136*
Bottigheimer, Ruth B.

137

boundary
1, 45, 52, 56, 57, 61, 67, 68, 88, 132
brother
39, 41, 62, 63, 64, 65, 67, 69, 70, *103, 105, 107, 115,* 120, 122, 123, 128, 134, *136, 138*
Brown, Norman O.
138
Burman, Erica
135
Campion, Jane
138
cannibalism
122, 123, 124
Carter, Angela
138
catastrophe
28, 29, 45, 60, 134
child
5, *11, 13, 15,* 17, 18, 19, 20, 22, 26, 29, 30, *83, 85,* 93, 96, 97, 98, *101, 103, 109,* 117, 118, 119, 120, 131, 132, *135, 136, 137*
childhood
2, 17, 18, 20, 31, 62, 93, 121, 131, *135, 136*
Chinen, A. B.
137
communication
1, 2, 15, 16, 19, 20, 22, 25, 52, 54, 55, 65, 69, 87, 89, 93, 121, *135*
consciousness
2, *41,* 45, 46, 50, 54, 57, 58, 59, 60, 63, 64, 66, 67, 69, 89
creativity
3, 18, 122, *135, 136, 138*
Dada
93
daughter
9, *11, 39,* 62, 63, 98, *103, 109,* 120, 121, 122

death
9, 19, 23, 28, 29, *35, 39,* 46, 50, 53, 54, 57, 59, 63, 68, 73, *75, 79, 81, 83,* 88, 89, 92, 93, 94, 95, 96, 98, *101, 113,* 119, 120, 121, 123, 126, 127, 128, 131, 134, *138*
desire
2, 25, 26, 27, 28, 29, 31, *37, 41,* 70, 77, 87, 89, 90, 91
development (human)
1, 2, 93, 128, 131, *135, 137*
devil
13, 17, 30, 31, 125, 126, 127
digestion
117, 118, 119, 120, 122, 123
dominance
3, 24, 48, 49, 50, 62, 63, 87, 119
dream
41, 58, 59, 60, 61, 62, 64, 65, 66, 67, 69, 117, 133, *135*
eating
2, *13, 35, 105,* 117, 118, 119, 123, 124, 126, 129
elimination
118, 119, 122, 124, 126, 127, 129, *138*
Ellis
135
Ellmann, Maud
138
emotion
26, 31, 45, 47, 54, 56, 57, 58, 63, 65, 69, 89, 123
error
21, 22, 26, 88, *117, 135, 136*
evil
11, 17, 28, *103,* 120, 121, 125, 126, 127, 128, 132, *136*
experience
1, 2, 16, 17, 18, 20, 21, 24, 25, 26, 27, 46, 48, 51, 53, 54, 60, 61, 62, 65, 69, 87, 89, 92, 93, 95, 97, 120, 121, 125, 131, 132, 133, 134, *135, 136, 137*
fairy tale

Index

15, 16, 22, 28, 47, 55, 62, 87, 91, 93, 132, 133, 134, *135, 136, 137, 138*
family
   18, 19, 21, 22, 62, 64, 67, 70, 87, 96, 98, 99, 117, 120, 122, 123, 129, 133, 134, *135, 137*
fate
   21, 29, *35, 37,* 51, 53, 58, 61, 62, 63, 66, 69, 89, 127
father
   5, 7, 9, 11, 21, 22, 23, 24, 26, 27, 28, 29, 30, 31, *73, 75, 83,* 88, 92, 96, 97, 98, *105, 107, 109, 111, 113, 115,* 119, 123, 124, 126, 127, 129, 132, 133
fear
   7, *33, 35,* 47, 48, 50, 51, 52, 54, 56, 65, 69, *103,* 120, 132
feeling
   2, *13,* 17, 19, 20, 21, 22, 26, 27, 28, *33, 35,* 46, 51, 52, 53, 55, 57, 59, 61, 62, 63, 64, 66, 67, *73, 77, 79,* 89, 92, 94, 97, 98, *100, 101, 103, 105, 107, 111, 113, 115,* 117, 121, 123, 126, 127, 128, 131, 132
fiction
   45, 59, 60, 90, *135*
fluidity
   1, 3, 24, 27, 45, 46, 69, 90, 91, 98
Freud, Sigmund
   135
fury
   2, 31, *35, 39, 81,* 98, 127, 133, *136*
future
   1, 30, 49, 64, 66, 69, 87, 88, 93
Grimm, Jacob and Wilhelm (Brüder/Brothers)
   4, 15, *32,* 47, *72,* 93, *100,* 119, 131, 132, *135, 136, 137, 138*
Grimm, Wilhelm
   52, 64
happiness
   5, 7, 9, 26, *43,* 45, 47, 61, 62, 63, 66, 70, *85,* 87, 98, *101, 105, 107, 111, 115,* 118, 126, 129, 131, 133

hearing
   3, 18, 22, 27, 68, 87, 125, 126, 132
heart
   5, 9, 15, 19, 25, 31, *37, 39,* 51, 55, 59, 62, 64, 66, 67, *75, 77, 79, 81, 85,* 93, 94, *101, 103,* 118, 133
Hirsh-Pasek, Kathy
   135
horror
   3, 21, 97, 127, 132
Hunt, Margaret
   136
Hunt, Peter L.
   135
husband
   17, 28, 30, *37,* 45, 69, 98, 99, *101*
identity
   25, 31, 50, 51, 69, 89, 120
idiom
   1, 2, 16, 48, 54, 87, 119
imagination
   1, 18, 47, 57, 64, 66, 93, 123, 124, 125, 128, 132, 133, 134, *137*
immediacy
   1, 3, 15, 18, 20, 51, 70, 93, 95, 123, 125/26, 128
incest
   63, 64, 70, 123, *137*
infanticide
   90, 132
interpretation
   1, 3, 16, 21, 45, 91, 131, 132
Kernberg, Otto
   136
king
   5, 9, 11, 13, 15, 16, 17, 18, 19, 20, 23, 27, 28, 29, 30, 31, *73, 75, 77, 79, 81, 83, 85,* 87, 88, 89, 90, 91, 92, 93, 94, 95, 96, 97, 98, 117, 119, 120, 122, 124, 125, 133
Klein, Melanie
   136
knowledge

49, 58, 59, 63, 96, 128

Kristeva, Julia
    136
Kudszus, W. G.
    136, 137
language
    1, 2, 3, 15, 16, 18, 19, 20, 21, 22, 23, 24,
    25, 26, 27, 45, 52, 54, 55, 58, 63, 66, 67,
    68, 87, 88, 89, 90, 91, 92, 93, 94, 95,
    119, 120, 121, 124, 125, 126, 132, *135,
    136*
Lesnik-Oberstein, Karín
    135
life
    1, *9*, 17, 25, 26, 27, 28, 29, 30, 31, *37*,
    49, 50, 51, 53, 57, 58, 61, 62, 63, 64, 65,
    66, 68, 70, 73, *75*, *81*, *83*, *85*, 89, 90, 93,
    94, 95, 96, 97, 98, 117, 119, 120, 121,
    122, 126, 128, 132, 133, *135, 138*
limit
    45, 48, 51, 52, 55, 56, 57, 92, 125, 128,
    132
linearity
    1, 2, 20, 21, 28, 54, 131, *135, 136*
listening
    2, 21, *37*, 52, *79*, 92, *136*
love
    3, 27, *37*, *39*, 61, 62, 63, 65, 67, 69, *73*,
    75, *79*, *83*, 88, 89, 93, 97, *101, 103*
luck
    33, 45, 47, 48, 49, 50, 51, 53, 54, 55, 57,
    59, 60, 62, 63, 65, 69, 70, 71, 77
Lüthi, Max
    136, 137
Lundell, Torborg
    138
magic
    18, 23, *39*, *43*, 70, *135*
Manheim, Ralph
    21, 24, 25, 48, 63, 94, 97, *136*
maternal

97, 98, 117, 121, 122, 123, 126, 127,
128, 132

McGlathery, James M.
    135, 137
membrane
    53, 55, 57, 58, 59, 133
memory
    16, 22, 26, 27, 28, 61, 62, 63, 89, 92, 94,
    99, 123, 125, 128, 134
Michnick Golinkoff, Roberta
    135
Miller, Alice
    15, *136*
Milosz, Czeslaw
    131
mother
    9, 28, 29, 31, 51, 87, 90, 94, 96, 97, 98,
    103, 105, 107, 109, 111, 113, 117, 119,
    120, 121, 122, 123, 124, 125, 127, 128,
    129, 133, *135, 137, 138*
multivalence
    15, 20, 23, 25, 28, 88, 91, 93, 95, 132
murder
    16, 98, 123, 126, 132
music
    39, *61*, 65, 66, *79*, 92
narrative
    1, 3, 15, 19, 20, 22, 25, 26, 27, 28, 30,
    31, 46, 47, 48, 50, 51, 52, 53, 54, 55, 62,
    63, 64, 65, 66, 67, 70, 87, 89, 90, 91, 92,
    93, 95, 96, 97, 117, 119, 120, 122, 123,
    124, 125, 126, 127, 128, 129, 131, 132,
    133, 134, *136, 137, 138*
nascency
    2, 93
nature
    53, 92, 125
nightmare
    39, 52, 61, 62, 64, 65, 66, 69, 70, *87*, 88,
    133
Ogden, Thomas H.
    137

Index

origins
  2, 94, 97, 121, 122, 126, *135*
passion
  73, 87, 89, 93, 94, 96, 98, 117, 131
past
  1, 16, 26, 28, 30, 31, 61, 65, 66, 87, 88, 92, 93, 95, 96, 97, 117, 119, 121, 126, 133
paternal
  24, 28, 29, 90
perception
  15, 20, 21, 25, 50, 55, 56, 57, 58, 59, 118, 120, 121, 131
periphery
  52, 56, 63, 64, 69
Perrault, Charles
  137
perspective
  1, 16, 22, 64, 96
Pessoa, Fernando
  61
Phillips, Adam
  135
play
  1, 2, 15, *83*, 96, 98, *135*
plot
  1, 3, 15, 20, 21, 25, 27, 28, 29, 30, 45, 50, 54, 58, 61, 64, 66, 67, 68, 87, 90, 91, 94, 95, 96, 99, 117, 119, 123, 131, 132, *136*
poetry
  66, 119, 122, 125, 127
Polívka
  138
pregnancy
  118, 119, 124, 125, 127
prelinguistic
  89, 90, 121, *135*
present
  1, 3, 16, 26, 28, 29, 31, 47, 61, 65, 70, 87, 95, 96, 97, 121, 123, 131
preverbal
  87, 132, 134

princess
  30, 73, *75, 77, 79*, 88, 90, 91, 92, 93, 94, 96, 133
promise
  3, *5, 7, 9, 11*, 21, 22, 23, 26, 27, 29, 30, *43*, 54, 55, 70, 71, *73, 75*, 88, 95, 132
psychosis
  18, 132, *136*
queen
  9, 11, 17, 27, 28, 29, *81, 83, 85*, 89, 94, 95, 96, 97, 98, 132
rage
  15, 16, 18, 28, 29, 31, *41*, 69
repetition
  27, 91, 95, 124, 127
rhythm
  46, 55, 93, *136*
Rölleke, Heinz
  136, 137
Rose, Jacqueline
  135
Runge, Daniel
  138
Runge, Philipp Otto
  138
Schectman, Jacqueline M.
  138
Schein
  3, *32, 38*, 50, 56, 66, 69, 89, 90, 91, 92, 95, 97, 98
Schlichting, Hans Burkhard
  137
self
  2, 3, 18, 19, 51, 87, 131, 133, *135*
Sharp, Daryl
  137
sign
  2, 30, 31, *35*, 46, 52, 54, 55, 56, 57, 58, 63, 64, 98
silence

7, 15, 27, 28, 29, 31, *39*, 45, 52, 58, 61, 65, 66, 68, *73*, *81*, 88, *105*, 122, 131, 133, *137*
sister
    26, 27, 63, 64, *107*, *109*, *111*, *113*, 124, 126, 129
skin
    45, 52, 53, 54, 55, 56, 57, 59, 61, 63, 65, 68, 69, 94, 133, 134, *137*
son
    7, *9*, *11*, 15, 16, 22, 23, 24, 28, 29, 30, 73, *83*, *85*, 88, 89, 93, 95, 98, *103*, *105*, 119, 121, 122, 123, 126, 128, 129, 133
sound
    1, 15, 28, *35*, *37*, *39*, 50, 55, 58, 62, 65, 70, 87, *101*, 118, 124, 125, 127, 128, 133
space
    2, 24, 25, 45, 50, 52, 53, 55, 56, 57, 59, 64, 68, 69, 77, 89, 90, 118, 123, 125, 127, 132, 133, *135*, *137*
speech
    1, 2, *9*, *13*, 15, 16, 17, 18, 19, 20, 21, 22, 23, 28, 29, *39*, *45*, 48, 49, 50, 51, 52, 54, 55, 58, 59, 61, 62, 63, 64, 66, 67, 68, 69, *75*, *83*, 87, 89, 90, 92, 93, 95, 96, 97, 117, 119, 121, 122, 123, 133, 134, *135*
spell
    7, 25, 26, 28, 66
splitting
    16, 17, 117, 120, 121, 125, 126, 128, *136*
Steig, Reinhold
    138
stepmother
    118, 120, 121, 122, 123, 124, 125, 126, 127, 128, 132, *138*
stepson
    120, 121, 122, 126
Stern, Daniel N.
    135
story

1, 3, 15, 19, 20, 21, 22, 24, 25, 27, 28, 29, 30, 31, *37*, 45, 48, 49, 50, 52, 54, 55, 56, 57, 58, 59, 60, 61, 62, 63, 64, 65, 66, 67, 68, 69, 70, 71, 87, 89, 91, 92, 93, 94, 95, 98, 117, 118, 119, 120, 122, 123, 125, 127, 128, 129, 131, 132, 133, 134, *136*
stranger
    39, *41*, 57, 58, 62, 63, 64, 65, 66, 67, 69, 77, 90, 92, 133, *137*
tailor
    33, *35*, *37*, *43*, 45, 46, 47, 48, 49, 50, 51, 52, 53, 54, 55, 56, 57, 58, 59, 61, 62, 63, 65, 66, 67, 68, 69, 70, 89, 133
tale
    1, 3, 15, 16, 17, 18, 19, 22, 24, 25, 26, 28, 29, 30, *39*, 45, 46, 47, 48, 49, 50, 52, 54, 55, 57, 59, 61, 62, 63, 64, 65, 66, 67, 68, 70, 71, 87, 88, 89, 90, 91, 92, 93, 95, 96, 98, 117, 118, 119, 121, 122, 123, 124, 125, 126, 127, 128, 129, 131, 132, 133, 134, *135*, *136*, *137*, *138*
Tatar, Maria
    136, *138*
terror
    15, 18, 27, 29, 31, 45, 46, 57, 58, 69, 70, 117, 126, 131, 132, 134
time
    1, 2, 3, *7*, *9*, 16, 17, 19, 21, 24, 27, 28, 29, 30, *35*, 45, 47, 48, 49, 51, 57, 59, 60, 65, 67, 73, *75*, *79*, *81*, *83*, 87, 88, 89, 90, 91, 92, 93, 94, 95, 96, 97, 98, *101*, 117, 118, 119, 120, 121, 126, 128, 132
toddler
    18, 19, 21, 24, 26, 31
torment
    7, 15, 18, 28, 61, 66, 91, 128
transformation
    1, 26, 28, *41*, 51, 56, 65, 67, 69, 95, 119, 124, 127, 128
transgression
    61, 64, 68, 69, 96
translation

15, 18, 19, 21, 24, 25, 26, 30, 46, 48, 63, 93, 94, *135, 136, 137*
trauma
    119, 125
Tustin, Frances
    137
uncertainty
    45, 46, 50, 51, 54, 58, 66, 68, 69, 70, 92
Uther, Hans-Jörg
    135, 136, 137
Venuti, Lawrence
    136
Versprechen
    4, 6, 8, *10*, 21, 22, 23, 25, 26, 27, 29, 30, 42, 70, 71, *72*, *74*, 88, 90, 93, 95, 97, 98, 99, *137*
violence
    31, 51, 53, 55, 56, 90, 91, 98, 118, 133, *136*
von Franz, Marie-Louise
    136
walking
    5, *11*, 19, 20, 24, 26, 27, 29, 30, 31, *33*, 54, *75*, *77*, *87*

wedding
    9, *13*, 16, 17, 28, 30, 70, *81*, 94, 95, 134
Wickes, Frances G.
    135
wife
    11, *13*, 16, 17, 26, 30, 31, *79*, *85*, 89, 98, *101*, *103*, *105*, *109*, *111*, *113*, *115*, 118, 119, 123
Winnicott, D. W.
    3, 133, *135, 136, 137*
Winterson, Jeanette
    87
wish
    2, *9*, *11*, *13*, 25, 28, 29, 30, 31, 88, 91, 93, 94, 98, *101*, 119, 120, 126, 127, 128
word
    1, 2, *9*, *11*, *13*, 15, 16, 17, 18, 19, 22, 23, 25, 26, 27, 28, 29, 30, *33*, *41*, *45*, 48, 52, 55, 57, 58, 61, 63, 65, 66, 67, 68, 69, 70, 75, *83*, *87*, 88, 89, 90, 91, 92, 93, 94, 98, *111*, 121, 124, 129, 132, 133, *135*
Zipes, Jack
    135, 136